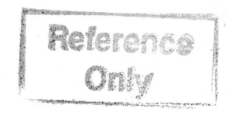

# bréifne

a different journey around
cavan, Leitrim, Fermanagh, Sligo and Roscommon

Cuilcagh Mountain dominates the skyline in Fermanagh and Cavan

# Bréifne

The landscapes of Bréifne are amongst the most unique in Ireland and the area has a rich culture and heritage. In recognition of these special features the local authorities in Cavan, Fermanagh, Leitrim, Sligo and Roscommon, along with the Geological Survey of Ireland, the Geological Survey of Northern Ireland, the University of Ulster and the Cavan County Enterprise Board have created this travel guide.

The name Bréifne is believed to have survived from a pre-Gaelic place name or population name. The *Metrical Dindshenchas* manuscript, originally collated before the end of the eleventh century, explained the origin of Bréifne thus:

**Bréifne, a brave soldier-woman**
**Daughter of Beoán MacBeothaigh**
**Fell in conflict about that land**
**With the children of Cámh by deceitful power**

This suggests that the land of Bréifne derived its name from the fallen soldier-woman. This explanation itself has literary origins going back to the eighth century.

The modern Irish spelling of the name is Bréifne. In Old Irish, Middle Irish and in later medieval sources the name is variously spelt as Breithne, Breifne, Brefne, Bréfne, Breithfne, Bréifne and Breibne. The territory of Bréifne was never constant and is believed to have been coextensive with the lands held by the O'Reilly and O'Rourke clans.

We hope you enjoy this different journey around Cavan, Leitrim, Fermanagh, Sligo and Roscommon.

**Contributors:** The directors of Bréifne, especially Vincent Reynolds (Chairman), Terry Egan, Pat O'Connor (Geological Survey of Ireland), Joanne Hayes (Cavan Tourism), Patrick McKeever (Geological Survey of Northern Ireland), Richard Watson (Fermanagh District Council), Ger Finn and Joe McLaughlin (Cavan County Council), Fionnuala Meagher (Sligo County Council), Martin Dolan (Leitrim County Council), Nollaig McKeown (Roscommon County Council), Professor Brian Graham (University of Ulster), Mary Mulvey (GreenBox) and Tanya Cathcart (Fermanagh Lakelands Tourism); and the Bréifne Project Team of Schalk van Lill, Chris McWilliams, Linda Shine, Sam Moore, Gráinne O'Shea, Koen Verbruggen, Fiona Dunne, Vincent Gallagher and Niamh Redmond.

**Managing editor:** Terry Egan
**Editorial consultancy and services:** Michael Johnston, Sheelagh Hughes,
Editorial Solutions, Belfast
**Photography:** Mike Bunn, Arrow Productions, Carrick-on-Shannon
**Design:** 2b-Creative, Lisburn
**Publisher:** The Stationery Office Ltd 2006

Printed in Northern Ireland by Graham and Heslip, Belfast

ISBN-10: 0-33-708747-4
ISBN-13: 978-033-708747-9

# Contents

Ballintempo Uplands and Cuilcagh Mountains

The Peace Memorial close to Senator George Mitchell Bridge on the road from Belturbet to Derrylin

# THE HISTORY OF BRÉIFNE

Bréifne has always been a secret place, a borderland between Ulster to the north, Connaught to the west and Leinster to the east, not quite part of one or the others – a place between and a place apart. It has always been a mysterious region, both remote and separate, and ruled by its own powerful families. We become familiar with these families only when they stray on to the broader stage of the political warfare that, for millennia, defined Ireland's history.

## Borderland

Borders separate, but at the same time borderlands are regions where different cultures intermingle. Bréifne has always been that kind of place and the borderland theme runs through its history as powerfully as the infant River Shannon drives south from its birthplace on the western slopes of Cuilcagh.

Much of Bréifne's history can only be glimpsed as shadows or distant echoes of the main events in Ireland's history. For, like other borderlands, Bréifne was remote from centres of power where the written records were made and kept. Within these lands the significant events of Irish history were played out – but took on their own particular meanings and resonances, shaped always by Bréifne's 'inbetweenness'.

Often a hard landscape, much of Bréifne has never been densely populated. We know of past peoples less from the written records they left behind than from the archaeological monuments that dot the landscape and the oral folk tales of their heroes and villains.

As if to add to the mystery, Bréifne's boundaries have changed through history, waxing and waning according to the success or failure of its ruling families in the endless dynastic and tribal warfares. The present counties of Cavan, Leitrim, Sligo, Roscommon and Fermanagh date only from the later sixteenth century, when they were set by the English administration in Ireland. But as has always been the case on the island, one set of boundaries has its precedents in older markers: Leitrim, Sligo and Roscommon once formed the northern borders of Connaught, Fermanagh the southern borders of Ulster, while Cavan has always looked north to Ulster but also east to the anglicised lands of eastern Leinster. The provinces today summarise the major dynastic territories of the first millennium AD, each with its array of tributary kingdoms.

King's Mountain and the passage to the sea was a strategic prize which the armies of Connaught and Ulster fought over

## Early Bréifne

We know little of early Bréifne people apart from their megalithic tombs, several of which still crown hilltops in the Bricklieve Mountains near Boyle and Knocknarea near Sligo. The locations of these ceremonial sites suggest, however, a people who had a special relationship with their place. The age of metal that followed – first bronze and then iron – remains but dimly visible through burial monuments and occasional archaeological finds.

The megalithic hilltop tomb on Knocknarea with Lough Gill in the foreground. The burial chambers of the early settlers are to be found all around Bréifne

**A Middle Bronze Age spearhead**

Image ©National Museum and Galleries of Northern Ireland

What we do have is a rich folklore that originates in the tales written down by monks in the seventh and eighth centuries. Significant among these are the stories of Bréifne interwoven into the *Táin Bó Cuailnge (The Cattle-raid of Cooley)*. This story, which is the central tale in the Ulster Cycle, the oldest and greatest of the four cycles of Irish mythology, records the rivalry between Ulster and Connaught.

In Ireland, the period between the fourth and the twelfth century is often labelled Early Christian, although perhaps its most important feature lay in the interconnections between the development of the church and the rise of political dynasties. Among the most powerful of these were the Uí Néill in Ulster and the Ua Conchobair in Connaught. The mountains and uplands of Bréifne acted as the frontier between the lands of the Airgialla and northern Uí Néill (O'Neill) in Ulster and the various branches of the Ua Conchobair (O'Connor) family in Connaught. Thus the narrow coastal gap west of Ben Bulben was a strategic prize which, historically, allowed mutual access to their rival territories for the armies of Connaught and Ulster. This is also the period when written records began and we can start to glimpse something of the life of Bréifne from documents as well as the landscape. Everything we know concerning the Early Christian period underscores the 'inbetweenness' of Bréifne. It was a contested land, which by the eighth century was substantially under the sway of the southern Uí Néill. Around this time , one of the Connaught dynastic

### Queen Maeve

The legendary Queen Maeve, ruler of Connaught from her royal dwelling at Rathcroaghan, is supposedly buried in Maeve's Cairn on the summit of Knocknarea 6km west of Sligo. It completely dominates the skyline in this part of Sligo. Maeve is said to be buried standing up in the cairn, dressed in armour with her sword and spear facing her Ulster enemies to the east. The cairn is 60m in diameter, 12m high and has a volume of 14,123m³ of stone. It probably covers a passage tomb dating to 3000 BC although it has never been excavated. The summit is a 45 minute walk from the carpark at the base of Knocknarea and spectacular views of the surrounding countryside can be enjoyed.
© Jim Fitzpatrick

kingdoms, that of the Uí Briúin, whose descendants became the O Raghailligh (O'Reillys), began to expand east of the Shannon into what was then a quite desolate and thinly populated terrain in Leitrim and Cavan.

We know little of this 'upstart kingdom' but it separated the Uí Néill lands in Ulster from the territories of their southern branch in the midlands. In 792, the first king of Bréifne to be named in the Irish Annals (a generic term to cover a whole set of medieval documents largely compiled by monastic scribes and generally referred to as the Irish Annals), Cormac Mac Dub-dá-Chrich, was killed in battle. Over the next three centuries complex political dynasties struggled with each other over the lands of Bréifne which, by the eleventh century, were under the control of the Ua Ruairc (O'Rourke) royal family.

## Medieval Bréifne

Although Bréifne suffered Viking raids on the monastic centres of Devenish and Inishmurray, it seems to have been largely unmarked by the Viking settlement in Ireland between the ninth and eleventh centuries. The attempted Anglo-Norman colonisation which began in the last three decades of the twelfth century had a much more substantial effect.

In 1186, one of the greatest of the Norman barons, Hugh de Lacy, was described in the Annals as King of Meath, Breffny and Uriel (modern Louth) and by the early thirteenth century, there seems to have been an Anglo-Norman attempt to colonise parts of Cavan and Leitrim. In 1220 Walter de Lacy led 'a great hosting' to the O'Reillys' crannóg (island fortress) somewhere on Lough Oughter near Cavan. These sporadic campaigns to establish a Norman presence in Bréifne seem to have soon petered out but still remain marked in the landscape by Norman earthwork castles.

Further west, after 1235, the Normans did enter and settle parts of Connaught including Sligo, where the Fitzgeralds built a castle c.1245. In north Roscommon, a campaign included the destruction of the Mac Dermott island fortress on *Loch Cé* (Lough Key) near Boyle.

At times, the O'Reillys did ally themselves to the Normans and were also later successful in annexing territory from the English to the east in Meath. To the west, however, the O'Connors and O'Rourkes, who had their chief seat at Dromahair, were more powerful. By the late fourteenth century, Bréifne had consolidated into two territories, the O'Rourke kingdom in the west (centred on modern Leitrim) and the O'Reilly kingdom to the east (largely modern Cavan).

## Fifteenth to nineteenth centuries

As borderland places these so-called 'Gaelic lordships' were marked by a combination of many

Devenish Island, scene of a Viking landfall in Fermanagh

A depiction of Irish 'woodkern' or light armed soldiers, drawn in 1580

influences. The O'Reilly lordship looked east to the English Pale around Dublin and its rulers seem to have understood the idea of a state. Cavan was developed as a market town in competition with the English of Meath.

Meanwhile, the O'Rourke lordship is less visible in the documents but it seems to have looked north, where the Maguires controlled the well-settled southern Fermanagh lakelands, and west towards the port of Sligo. Thus the wild and empty mountain lands stretching from Cuilcagh to Slieve Anierin above Drumshanbo separated the two Bréifnes just as the range linking Cuilcagh and Ben Bulben marked Bréifne

off from Ulster. During the sixteenth century, English administrative control gradually extended over Bréifne. Cavan and Fermanagh were included in Ulster after the demarcation of county boundaries, while the remainder of the region was part of Connaught. Thus, Cavan and Fermanagh, but not Leitrim, Sligo or Roscommon, were included in the Ulster Plantations of 1609-13, the English and Scottish colonisation that followed the Flight of the Earls in 1607. The colonisation is still marked in the landscape by the planters' castles such as Monea and Tully in south Fermanagh. Although interrupted by the 1641 Rebellion, the plantations led directly to the social

reconstruction in Ireland that followed the Cromwellian era in the 1650s. This saw the massive expropriation of land and the resettlement of native Irish. Many of the Irish landholders in Bréifne were dispossessed and their lands reallocated to ex-Cromwellian soldiers and adventurers.

As elsewhere in Ireland, this land reallocation laid the basis for the environmental revolution of the eighteenth and early nineteenth centuries. The human landscape was transformed as newly empowered landlords laid out estates centred on 'big' houses and improved existing or created new towns and villages.

It is difficult to differentiate between these events in Bréifne and elsewhere in Ireland. The region seems to have been largely quiescent during the eighteenth and early nineteenth centuries. It was little affected by the 1798 Rebellion although the French expedition under General Humbert, which landed at Killala Bay in Co Mayo, having defeated the Sligo militia at Collooney, did pass through Glenade and Manorhamilton on its way to eventual surrender near Longford.

At this time the economy was based on simple agriculture – oats, potatoes and livestock – while the new towns and villages were often laid out with wide main streets which doubled up as livestock markets. The only substantial industry was textile manufacturing and there were many small mills.

## Eoghan Rua Ó Néill

Born in Co Tyrone around 1597, Eoghan Roe (Ruadh, the red-complexioned) was the son of Art MacBaron O'Neill and the nephew of Hugh O'Neill, Earl of Tyrone. As a young soldier he distinguished himself in the Spanish-French War by holding out for 48 days with a mere 2,000 men against a French army of 35,000. When the Irish rebelled against the planters in 1641 Eoghan Roe returned to Ulster and was welcomed by the O'Reillys of Bréifne. In 1646 he led an army to victory against the English at Benburb, afterwards returning to Cavan. A few years later he fell ill and died at Clough Oughter Castle. Under cover of night he was buried in the Franciscan Abbey in Cavan town. His death was a colossal blow to the Irish of Ulster and was kept secret for some time.

The iron industry around Lough Allen, which had begun c.1600, was a notable exception to the reliance on agriculture and agricultural products. Despite this modest economy, the population of parts of Bréifne was growing fast in the early nineteenth century, the highest rates being in Leitrim, Sligo and north Roscommon. Emigration to the New World was one response but population growth in the region was halted by the Great Famine of 1845-1849. Indeed, until the early twenty-first century, the population of much of Bréifne has continued to decline: Leitrim, for example, had 155,000 people in 1841 compared to just over 25,000 today.

## Estate towns

**Fair day in Ballinamore circa 1950**          Image ©National Library of Ireland

During the eighteenth century many towns were established or improved by landlords of large estates. The towns frequently had a similar plan, which was dominated by a long, often widened street ending in a market place that usually had a courthouse or a market house as its architectural focus. Towns such as Boyle and Dromahair are good examples of how urban improvement and planning was carried out in the eighteenth and nineteenth centuries. Other examples include Manorhamilton, Belturbet, Kinlough, Ballyconnell, Belleek and Ballymote. In many cases the tenants carried out the modernisation of the towns, with the landlord co-ordinating the work and providing the incentive.

## The Battle of Carricknagat and Union Wood

A life-sized figure of Bartholomew Teeling stands on the road (R290) outside Collooney. The Teeling Monument was erected in 1898 to commemorate the 1798 French invasion force, under General Humbert, that landed in Killala Bay, to assist in the 1798 Irish Rebellion. The French were halted here by an English force which had installed cannon on Union Rock, the rocky outcrop to the west. Captain Bartholomew Teeling was an Irishman serving in the French Army and was captured and later executed after the French were defeated at Ballinamuck, Co Longford.

**The Bartholomew Teeling 1798 memorial**

In the aftermath of the Famine, the principal victims of which were the poorest cottiers and farm labourers, livestock farming took over, not just throughout Bréifne but also in many other parts of Ireland. The number of small holdings declined dramatically and, despite continued emigration, there was a modest economic recovery. In the little towns and villages that became the centres of this economy, the middle class that emerged during these years became politicised during the 1880s and 1890s as the campaign for home rule in Ireland began to escalate. Again, Bréifne occupied a borderland location, the principal opposition to home rule coming from Ulster, the only part of Ireland to have become significantly industrialised, and which also had a Protestant majority.

## The twentieth century

By the first two decades of the twentieth century Irish nationalism was being contested between constitutional nationalists, who favoured home rule, and a more militant separatist wing, whose goal of independence led to the 1916 Easter Rising. If unsuccessful in itself, the Rising was still the precursor to the events that led to the creation of the Irish Free State, but also partition. While much of Bréifne was substantially Republican with high levels of Sinn Féin membership, Fermanagh, although it had a Catholic majority, was included in Northern Ireland under the Government of Ireland Act of 1920.

When partition took place in 1921, the 'inbetweenness' of the historic borderland of Bréifne was codified into a political boundary.

The Cenotaph in Enniskillen commemorates the fallen soldiers of the British Army

By 1923, there were custom posts on the major roads between Fermanagh and the rest of Bréifne at Belleek, Blacklion and Swanlinbar and even on the Sligo-Enniskillen railway line at Glenfarne. The population had to get used to different patterns of movement, including smuggling, a particularly active cross-border pastime during World War II. The war touched Bréifne through the military bases set up around Lough Erne, from which British and American flying boats operated to protect the North Atlantic convoys and search for U-boats.

In the last decades of the twentieth century, Bréifne's role as a borderland was again accentuated by the Troubles in Northern Ireland. Border crossings were closed and movement was channelled along the main roads and through frequent security checks.

At the same time, however, the entry of the United Kingdom and the Republic of Ireland to the European Union in 1973 began to open up new opportunities for cross-border co-operation, as did the funding later made available under the EU Peace and Reconciliation programmes. One of the most impressive results has been the reopening of the Shannon-Erne Waterway, which defines the southern boundary of Bréifne.

Today, Bréifne is still a place between and a place apart. Its mountains dominate the skyline looking south from Northern Ireland and north from the lowlands of Longford, Roscommon and east Sligo in the Republic of Ireland. Beyond the vibrancy of Bréifne's gateway towns like Boyle, Cavan, Carrick-on-Shannon and Enniskillen, lies a landscape in which history is everywhere. Bréifne is not timeless but it exudes the passage of time and the quiet ways in which the lives of ordinary people have been lived against the canvas of Irish history.

President Clinton opens the Clinton Centre in Enniskillen

The political turmoil of the time is captured in the pages of the *Impartial Reporter* and *Farmers Journal*.

## Seán Mac Diarmada

© National Museum of Ireland

Patriot and revolutionary

The loft bedroom in Mac Diarmada's cottage

All year by appointment.
**T:** 00353 (0)71 9853249

Sean Mac Diarmada (1884-1916), a leading Irish revolutionary and one of the seven signatories to the 1916 Proclamation of the Republic, was born in Corranmore, Kiltyclogher. He was one of ten children of Donald and Mary McDermott and studied Gaelic and bookkeeping near Dowra. When his chosen career as a teacher failed to materialise he spent time as a gardener in Scotland. He returned to Belfast in 1902 to take up employment as a tram driver.

Mac Diarmada joined the Irish Republican Brotherhood (IRB) in 1906 and served as Treasurer of the Supreme Council. The following year he became a full-time organiser for Sinn Féin and travelled the country setting up branches. The 1908 Parliamentary election saw Sinn Féin make an initial entry into politics in Mac Diarmada's heartland of north Leitrim.

He subsequently became manager of the *Irish Freedom Journal*. In 1912 he developed polio, which inhibited his travel around the roads of Ireland. In 1915 Mac Diarmada was elected to the Military Council of the IRB, which had the specific task of planning the Rising, and he was a very close ally of Thomas Clarke, the first signatory to the Proclamation of the Republic.

During Easter week 1916 he fought in the General Post Office. He was court-martialled, sentenced to death and executed on 12 May 1916. Mac Diarmada's remains lie in Arbour Hill Cemetery, Dublin. In 1940 a statue to his memory was erected in Kiltyclogher.

The family home is in the care of the Republic of Ireland's Office of Public Works and is signposted on approach roads to Kiltyclogher. The house is open to the public and access is arranged at the property itself. The location is a poignant reminder of life during the late nineteenth and early twentieth centuries and there is memorabilia on show from the McDermott family.

**Sean Mac Diarmada's family home at Kiltyclogher**

THE IMPARTIAL ... VEMBER 24, 1921

...nagh Co. Council

...managh Co. Council.

...els Against Authority.

...E SEIZE THE COURTHOUSE.

...sses Allegiance to Dail Eireann.

...DEACON TIERNEY MAKES PROTESTS

...F. Majority consists of.

## Great houses of Bréifne

The great houses of Ireland provide an insight into the social and political history of the country. In Bréifne good examples of these are the eighteenth century Florence Court House and Castle Coole, both near Enniskillen, and Lissadell House outside Sligo. The latter was the home of wealthy landowners, the Gore-Booths, and is intrinsically linked with the lives of celebrated poet W B Yeats and Irish revolutionary Constance Markievicz. Both Florence Court and Castle Coole are National Trust properties in Northern Ireland and open to the public, while Lissadell is a private family home in the Republic of Ireland with select opening times.

### Lissadell House

⚜ Ballinfull, Co Sligo
**T:** 00353 (0)71 9163150
**E:** info@lissadellhouse.com
**W:** lissadellhouse.com
**Open:** 16 March to 30 September, 10.30 am to 6pm.

♿ 🚹 ❄ 🍴 € 📷 Ⓟ 🔒

Few houses in Ireland can lay claim to the romantic, revolutionary and artistic connections of Lissadell House. The house was the childhood home of 'the Countess of Irish Freedom' Constance Markievicz as well as her sister Eva Gore – Booth, suffragette and poet. Lissadell was also the inspirational retreat of the poet W B Yeats and his brother, the painter Jack B Yeats.

The house was built in 1833 by Sir Robert Gore-Booth and designed by Francis Goodwin in the Greek revival style. The

Lissadell House has connections to many of the formative influences in the recent history of Ireland

### Florence Court House

⚜ Florencecourt, Enniskillen Co Fermanagh **T:** 0044 (0)28 6634 8249 **W:** nationaltrust.org.uk **E:** florencecourt@nationaltrust.org.uk
**Open:** March-September 1pm to 6pm **Grounds open all year:** Apr-Oct 10am to 8pm rest 10am to 4pm

♿ 🚹 ❄ 🏠 🍴 ✕ Ⓟ ℹ ♿ ♻ £ 📷

Located in Florencecourt village near Blacklion and Belcoo, Florence Court House is set in beautiful Fermanagh countryside and is one of the most important houses in the north-west. It is romantically named after the wife of Sir John Cole who first built a

house on this spectacular site in the early eighteenth century. The present Palladian style house was probably built by his son John, afterwards the first Lord Mount Florence.

The wings and pavilion were added to the mid eighteenth-century block around 1770 by William Cole, the first Earl of Enniskillen and may have been designed by Davis Ducart. The rest of the house and the striking rococo plasterwork after the manner of Robert West have been meticulously restored. Family pictures and historic items owned by the sixth Earl of Enniskillen have been returned to Florence Court in accordance with his wishes, and are on display in

the house. The beautiful grounds present the opportunity for a serene walk. The original Irish yew, from which all upright Irish yews were propagated, is in the grounds. The house tour includes viewing the exquisite rococo decoration, fine Irish furniture and service quarters.

The rococo plasterwork is a feature of the house

Florence Court was built in the mid eighteenth century with arcades and pavillions added later

conservative tastes of both patron and architect resulted in the adoption of a chaste neo-classical design – the last time this style was used for a large country house in Ireland. The exterior walls of grey Ballysadare limestone

incorporate very little ornament apart from corner pilasters and a strong horizontal frieze. As boys the Yeats brothers visited Lissadell for cricket matches and horse racing. As a young man the poet made friends with Constance and Eva, and stayed

at Lissadell during the years 1894 and 1895. Today the house is in private ownership and there is an extensive restoration programme underway with a particular focus on the gardens and woodlands surrounding the house. Guided tours are available.

The Great Hall at Lissadell with its meticulously restored 1890s' Danish Crown salon stove

The dining room.at Lissadell

## Castle Coole

Enniskillen, Co Fermanagh
**T:** 0044 (0)28 6632 2690
**E:** castlecoole@nationaltrust.org.uk **W:** nationaltrust.org.uk
**Information Centre**
**Open:** March - September
**Opening hours:** 1pm to 6pm
**Grounds open all year:** Apr-Oct 10am to 8pm rest 10am to 4pm

Located on the outskirts of Enniskillen, Castle Coole was

designed by James Wyatt and completed in 1798 for the first Earl of Belmore. Castle Coole's interior was created by some of the leading craftsmen of the eighteenth century. Marble chimney-pieces were carved by Westmacott, plasterwork created by Joseph Rose and the scagioli columns are the work of Bartoli. Magnificent state rooms with their sumptuous Regency furnishings include the state bedroom prepared for a visit by George IV in 1821. The surrounding 700-acre estate is a fitting setting for the mansion with parkland, Lough Coole and extensive woods. There are enjoyable walks through the Grand Yard, the servants' quarters and tunnel and an ice house. The original Belmore Coach can also be viewed. Check directly with the property regarding events, music and recitals. The house is only a short drive or walk outside Enniskillen.

The dining room designed and furnished by James Wyatt

The Bow Room with its Chinese style wallpaper and early nineteenth centry satinwood furniture

The state bedroom at Castle Coole
Castle Coole Images ©National Trust

Castle Coole is possibly the finest neoclassical house in Ireland

# 7. Clough Oughter Castle

The castle is a short drive from Cavan town on the Killashandra road. It is a circular tower standing on a crannóg, or man-made island, which seems to have been built specifically to hold the castle. Clough Oughter was probably built by the Anglo-Norman William 'Gorm' de Lacy in the early thirteenth century. The O'Reillys, the leading Irish clan in the area, gained control of Clough Oughter in 1233 and retained control until the sixteenth century. During this time the castle was an important O'Reilly fortress and prison with Bishop Bedell (see p21) among those held there. It remained in their control until the Plantation of Ulster when it was made a royal castle. Recaptured by the O'Reillys in 1641 it was here that Eoghan Roe O'Neill, one of the great Irish chieftains, died in 1649. Clough Oughter Castle was badly damaged in 1653 during a Cromwellian siege and subsequently abandoned. The castle can be clearly appreciated from the shore, and is also accessible by boat, which can be hired locally.

# CAVAN - BELTURBET - BALLYCONNELL

## Cavan

Cavan is the only surviving town in Ireland established by a native Irish family (the O'Reillys, see p30), rather than by Anglo-Norman or Norse settlers. It grew up around a castle and a Franciscan friary built by the O'Reilly clan. By the end of the fourteenth century it was a thriving market town attracting merchants from as far as Dublin and Drogheda.

Over the last 20 years the town has prospered and has become an important shopping, tourism and business centre.

Cavan, or in Gaelic, *An Cabhán* (The Hollow), nestles between two drumlins. To the north and west lie the distinctive 'basket of eggs' drumlin country of bogs and small lakes, while to the south and east the land rises into low rolling hills.

The town has many fine buildings, friendly pubs, restaurants, shops and amenities. As a

The coarse and game fishing in Cavan's water systems is internationally renowned

gateway town, it is an excellent base for exploring Bréifne and, with its large network of lakes and waterways, is recognised as the home of coarse and game fishing in Ireland.

The county has a proud tradition in Gaelic football, and with 39 victories holds the record for winning the most Ulster senior

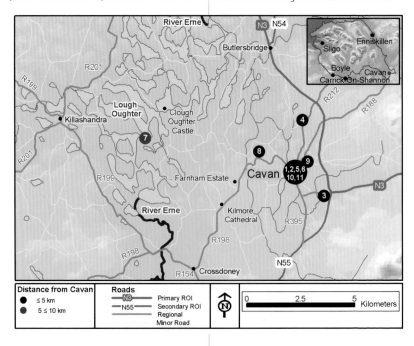

Taking a stroll on Bridge Street in Cavan town

## Radisson SAS Farnham Estate Hotel

T: 00353 (0)49 4377700
W: farnham.radissonsas.com

football titles. Cavan is served by excellent national routes. It is located less than two hours drive from Dublin and Belfast. It is connected to Dublin via the main N3 route which continues on to Enniskillen and then joins the A4 to Belfast. From Belfast take the M1 to the A3 and then the N54 in the Republic of Ireland.

## Accommodation and eating out

The four-star Radisson resort offers championship golf, conference facilities, a 3,7116sq m wellness centre, restaurants and extensive walking, trekking and fishing opportunities. The Farnham Arms Hotel on Cavan's main

street offers homely accommodation and regular entertainment in the hotel bar. The three-star Hotel Kilmore has recently been refurbished, while nearer to town the four-star Cavan Crystal Hotel is very contemporary in outlook but traditional in warmth and welcome. It offers full health and fitness facilities.

Restaurants in town include the Oak Room on Main Street, the Side Door, Sajan, Little Sicily, The Big Apple, The Bridge and the Bramley. Many pubs also serve food. Opus One is an award-winning restaurant within the Cavan Crystal Hotel. Great food is also available at the Annalee Restaurant in the Hotel Kilmore.

Situated in the elegant sixteenth-century Farnham Estate on the outskirts of Cavan town, the Radisson SAS Farnham Estate was the first destination lifestyle resort developed in the Republic of Ireland. Comprising 1,300 acres, the estate was home to the Farnham family for some 300 years. A large number of original features survive in the surrounding landscape, including workers' cottages, a deer park and an area of woodland. Hotel facilities include angling, horse riding, walking and an 18-hole golf course. The leisure centre has indoor and outdoor swimming pools, sauna, steam room and fitness suite. The 158 bedrooms and suites are all designed to reflect the estate's unique heritage. Eight of the suites are located in the original Farnham House. The hotel has a spa and wellness centre and a complete range of therapies are available. There are several bar and restaurant choices within the estate.

Top class dining can be enjoyed in Cavan

The Cavan Crystal Hotel has great leisure facilities

## Information point

### 1. Cavan Tourist Office
*i* Johnston Central Library and Farnham Centre
Farnham Street
T: 00353 (0)49 4331942
W: cavantourism.com
**Open:** Seasonal

### 2. St Mary's Abbey
[icons] Located on Abbey Street in Cavan town the abbey was originally built by the O'Reillys in 1300. A three-storey bell tower and a graveyard from this important Franciscan friary still remain.The friary was rebuilt many times in the following two centuries following damage in wars and fire. A plaque on the wall of the tower commemorates Eoghan Roe O'Neill, commander of the Catholic forces in Ireland, who was interred here after his death in 1649. Although their graves are no longer visible, many prominent members of the O'Reilly family are also buried here.

### 3. Cavan Crystal Showroom
T: 00353 (0)49 4331800
W: cavancrystaldesign.com
**Open:** All year
[icons] Established in 1969, Cavan Crystal is famous the world over. The factory is no longer open for tours, but visitors can explore the extensive showroom, which also displays and sells the work of local artists.

### John Joe O'Reilly

John Joe O'Reilly 1918-1952 is widely regarded as the greatest centre-half back in the history of Gaelic football. A native of Killashandra, near Cavan town, he played his early football with the nearby Cornafean club and St Patrick's College. After joining the Irish Army, he played with the Curragh team in Kildare in 1937. Affectionately known as 'Gallant John Joe', he played with Cavan from 1937 until the early 1950s, participating in six all-Ireland finals. His greatest achievement was captaining the Cavan team in beating Kerry in the famed 1947 all-Ireland final, played in the Polo Grounds, New York. In 1999, he was nominated at centre-half back in the An Post-GAA Team of the Millennium. John Joe is buried in Killashandra.

### 4. Cavan Equestrian Centre
T: 00353 (0)49 4332017
W: cavanequestrian.com
**Open:** All year
[icons] This holds showjumping events of national and international reputation and is one of Europe's leading horse and pony sales and marketing centres. There are over 400 stables, two indoor arenas, a large all-weather arena, four grass arenas and restaurant and bar facilities with saddlery and equestrian clothing shops.

### 5. Cavan Genealogical Centre
T: 00353 (0)49 4361094
W: cavangenealogy.com
**Open:** All year
[icons] There are over one million computer records relating to individuals who resided in Cavan, with the earliest church records dating from 1702. There is also a well stocked souvenir shop.

### 6. The Cathedral of St Patrick and St Feidhlim
With its 68m spire and flanking domes, the Roman Catholic cathedral is the most dominant building in Cavan town. Completed in 1942, the vast interior is styled like a basilica and extensive use is made of different colours of marble. The cathedral houses many fine examples of ecclesiastical art.

## Kilmore Cathedral and Motte and Bailey

Famous for its Romanesque doorway, the church first established at Kilmore in 885 did not become a cathedral until 1454. A tree-lined avenue now leads to this late medieval cathedral and the nineteenth-century Church of Ireland cathedral that replaced it. This later cathedral was designed by the English architect, William Slater, and dates to 1860. It features attractive stained glass windows depicting biblical scenes. The cathedral was intended as a memorial to Bishop Bedell, who was Bishop of Kilmore from 1629 to 1642 and whose grave is in the cathedral grounds. Bishop

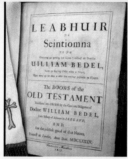

Bedell made a significant contribution to the Gaelic language by translating the Old Testament into Irish. His bible remained the standard Gaelic copy until the twentieth century and an original copy is on display in the cathedral.

The Romanesque doorway dates to the late twelfth or early thirteenth century, and is believed to have originally been part of the nearby priory at Trinity Island on Lough Oughter (see p46). The doorway is widely treasured as a priceless relic from the finest period of native Irish architecture.

Situated to the south of the cathedral is a circular covered holy well dedicated to St Feidhlim whose feast day occurs on 9 August. It probably dates to the seventeenth or eighteenth century. Opposite the main entrance door to Kilmore Cathedral are the remnants of a motte and bailey. There is no public access but the site can be viewed from the cathedral. This motte and bailey, similar to that at Turbet Island, was constructed by Walter de Lacy in 1211 as part of a series of seven fortifications built to secure a roadway to isolate this part of Ulster, which was then still under Irish control.

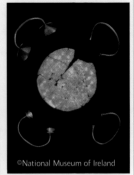

©National Museum of Ireland

**The Lattoon hoard is almost 3,000 years old**

©Irish Bird Images

The great crested grebe in its striking summer plumage. It breeds throughout the lake system of Lough Oughter

### 7. Killykeen Forest Park and Lough Oughter

The picturesque mixed woodland of Killykeen Forest Park overlooks Lough Oughter. Owned by the Republic of Ireland's national forestry agency Coillte, the park has a swimming area, although lifeguards are not always on duty. The waters are renowned for coarse angling with bream, roach, perch and pike being the main catches. The lake is an important over-wintering site for birds, particularly whooper swans, which gather in huge numbers, having flown from Iceland to escape the Arctic winter. Tufted duck, great crested grebe, cormorant, snipe, lapwing and golden plover can also be seen.
The elusive otter is also present and although seldom seen, tracks and feeding signs are evident. Extensive paths and nature trails through Killykeen Forest Park allow visitors to experience the wildlife of this area. The site as a whole is the best inland example of a flooded drumlin landscape in Ireland.

### Golf

### 8. County Cavan Golf Club

Founded in 1894, County Cavan Golf Club is one of the oldest in Ireland. The 18-hole, par 70 parkland course measures 5,634m.

The Erne Waterway Golf Championship is a three-day golf competition held annually in June and played over three parkland courses - the Slieve Russell in Cavan, Enniskillen and Castle Hume. The championship is open to all players holding official handicaps. Details of the current competition are available from the local tourism office or cavantourism.com

Among the most important archaeological finds in Cavan were the Crossdoney Lunula and the Lattoon hoard. The Crossdoney Lunula was discovered in a bog near Crossdoney outside Cavan town, at a depth of 2m and in an oak case. Lunulae are gold personal ornaments dating to the Early Bronze Age (c.2000 BC). They are made of thinly beaten sheets of gold fashioned into crescent shapes. It was acquired by the National Museum in 1884. The Lattoon hoard of gold ornaments was found deep in a bog at Lattoon, near Ballyjamesduff in 1919. This hoard consisted of two dress-fasteners, two bracelets and a disc of fine gold foil. The disc is decorated with concentric circles, hatched triangles and herringbone patterns. It would originally have covered a disc of copper or bronze. This hoard has been dated to the Later Bronze Age, 900-700 BC.
Both finds are now on display in an exhibition entitled 'Or, Ireland's Gold' at the National Musuem in Kildare Street, Dublin.

**The Crossdoney Lunula**

Image ©National Museum of Ireland

Foxgloves in bloom at Lough Oughter

## Percy French

Percy French (1854–1920) was a noted songwriter, performer and painter, born in Cloonyquin, Co Roscommon. He was employed by the Board of Works in Cavan as Surveyor of Drains and having left there in 1887 he embarked upon a successful song writing career. Among his most memorable songs are 'Come Back Paddy Reilly to Ballyjamesduff', 'Phil the Fluter's Ball', 'Slattery's Mounted Foot', 'The Mountains of Mourne' and 'Are Ye Right There, Michael?' The quality of these compositions established him as a stylish entertainer of note. In his lifetime he toured England, Canada, the USA and the West Indies. He is buried in Formby, near Liverpool in northern England.

## Traditional music

There are traditional music sessions throughout the year. The Full Schilling and Cathal Brady's in Cavan on Monday/Tuesday; in the Farnham Arms Hotel in Cavan on Wednesday nights; in Maggie's Bar in Killeshandra, The Angler's Rest Bar in Ballyconnell and The Black House Inn in Cavan on a Thursday; on Friday in the Yukon Bar in Belturbet; on Saturday nights in the Shamrock Inn , Killeshandra, The Swan Bar and the Welcome Inn in Swanlinbar and on Sunday nights in the Widow's in Belturbet.

Fleadh Cheoil an Cabháin takes place over a long weekend in June. A traditional Irish music festival, the fleadh has recently been held in the towns of Killashandra, Ballinagh and Cavan. The fleadh celebrates Irish music and dancing and features music competitions and many spontaneous music sessions in local pubs.

## Sport and leisure

The leisure centre in Cavan incorporates a 25m pool, gym, steam room, sauna, jacuzzi and restaurant. The town's six-screen cinema is open every day and beside it there is a six-lane bowling alley with children's bumpers, pool tables, video amusements and jukebox. Light refreshments are available. There is also good shopping in the adjacent streets.

**9. Cavan Pool and Leisure Complex**
T: 00353 (0)49 4362888

**10. Astra Bowl**
T: 00353 (0)49 4372662
W: astra-bowl.com

**11. Storm Cinema**
T: 00353 (0)49 4372020

Traditional music is very popular throughout Cavan and attracts all age groups to sessions

# Belturbet

Belturbet is perched on top of a drumlin on the eastern bank of the River Erne, against a backdrop of rolling hills dominated by Slieve Rushen. It is a Plantation town planned by Sir Stephen Butler after 1610 and laid out in a typical formation with a town hall at its head and two intersecting streets at right angles. The thirteenth-century motte and bailey on Turbet Island was probably the first major settlement at Belturbet. This was one of

The bridge over the Erne in Belturbet

Belturbet was a vital rail link in the north-west of Ireland

Image ©National Library of Ireland

seven fortifications built by the Anglo-Normans to isolate that part of Ulster still under native Irish control. It was abandoned by 1233 and was taken over by the O'Reillys who built a stone castle on the site.

The town's Gaelic name is *Béal Tairbirt*, (Mouth of the Isthmus), possibly referring to Turbet Island.

Belturbet's position on the Erne meant that historically it was an important centre of inland navigation, trade and conflict. By the early twentieth century Belturbet was a thriving market town. It was an important regional transportation hub and the point where the Cavan-Leitrim Railway met the Great Northern Railway. The former was a narrow-gauge

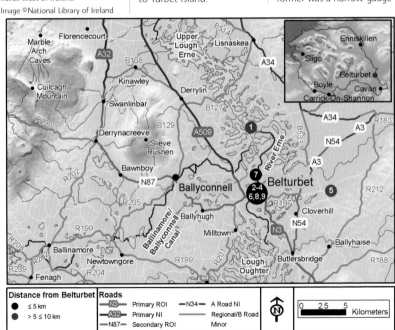

| Distance from Belturbet | Roads | | | |
|---|---|---|---|---|
| ● ≤ 5 km | N3 Primary ROI | N34 A Road NI | | |
| ● > 5 ≤ 10 km | A32 Primary NI | Regional/B Road | | |
| | N87 Secondary ROI | Minor | | |

0  2.5  5 Kilometers

Main Street, Belturbet

line that served the routes from Drumshanbo and Arigna and from Dromod; the latter was a standard-gauge railway running from Cavan to Clones and beyond. Passengers, goods, livestock, coal – whatever the cargo, it had to change trains at Belturbet.

In Victorian times Belturbet was the starting point for steamboat cruises along the Erne. Today it remains a prominent location for cruising, fishing and fun along the Erne and the network of lakes in the area. The reopening of the Shannon-Erne waterway in the 1990s invigorated the tourism potential of the town and it continues to attract visitors from Ireland and abroad. The area is a magnet for anglers as there is a variety of catch to be had in the local waters.

Belturbet is located 17km from Cavan town and 35km from Enniskillen, two gateway towns to Bréifne.

The Seven Horseshoes Hotel is located on the main street

## Accommodation and eating out

The Seven Horseshoes Hotel is located on the main street and has a long history dating back to horse and coach travel. Self-catering town houses are available in the town, as are the chalets of the International Fishing Centre on the River Erne. Several homely B&Bs, country houses and traditional farmhouses offering tourist accommodation can also be found within a short distance of the town. For eating out there is The Olde Post Inn, a family run restaurant, which has won numerous awards and has earned a reputation for fine food and genuine hospitality. The Seven Horseshoes is popular with boating folk. The restaurant of the International Fishing Centre is open to non-residents, providing French style cuisine. There is also the Captain's Table which offers contemporary cuisine.

## The Erne cot

George Morrissey

One of the greatest influences on life and the landscape in Bréifne is the River Erne. For many generations the traditional Erne cot was used to navigate the waterways and islands of the Erne system. Records of its use in everyday life go back as far as the fifteenth century. George Morrissey lives on the banks of the Erne in Belturbet and he, along with others, use their collective craftmanship to keep alive the image of the Erne Cot.

Traditionally made from an oak log the Erne Cot had blunt ends curved upwards both fore and aft, a flat base, and no keel. The vessel was particularly suited to travel over flooded land. For centuries the cot transported people, animals, produce, machinery and foodstuffs, providing a vital access link for the region and its inland islands. Weddings, funerals, dances and social visits all used the Erne cot as a means of transport. It is said the cot was also a favoured vessel of smugglers.

The family version was typically around 6m long, and required regular maintenance and a skilled and crafty oarsman. The vessels were last in common use during the late 1930s, and became a fading memory with the introduction of the car. While we will no longer see sights like the 1,500 war cots of the Maguire chieftains along the Erne, we can still cherish the role the vessel played in the history and life of all those who inhabit this part of Bréifne.

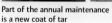

Part of the annual maintenance is a new coat of tar

The Erne Cot was once the primary means of travel on the river

## Information point

### 🛈 Cavan Tourist Office
Farnham Street, Cavan
**T:** 00353 (0)49 4331942
**W:** cavantourism.com
**Open:** Seasonal

### 1. Crom Estate
🎿♿🥾☸☕🍴£ 🅲🅲🅿🚗🛈🚴🎣♿
**T:** 0044 (0)28 6773 8118
**W:** nationaltrust.org.uk
This National Trust property, 7km from Belturbet, is an important nature reserve situated along the shores of Upper Lough Erne. There are well-maintained nature trails, one of the largest areas of oak woodland in Bréifne and historic ruins. The estate is also home to fallow deer, pine marten and a large heronry. There is also a wildlife exhibition and visitors can take part in a night-time bat walk. Holiday cottages and boats are available for hire and there is a fine visitor centre.

### 2. Turbet Island
♿🏛 The still discernable and interesting historic fortifications on Turbet Island are evidence that this river crossing was once of strategic importance. The thirteenth-century motte and bailey on the island was probably the first major settlement at Belturbet. A footbridge on the northern side leads to the island and there is an adjacent carpark.

### 3. Belturbet Church of Ireland
♿🏛 The church was built around 1828 within a star-shaped fort, which dates from 1689. The interior has plaster vaulting and mid-eighteenth-century monuments to a local family, the Whytes of Redhills. These forts were designed as a response to the development of artillery and provided a low target and wide banks to absorb the impact of canon fire.

## Festivals and other activities

### 4. Belturbet Golf Club
**T:** 00353 (0)49 9522287

### 5. Redhills Equestrian Centre
**T:** 00353 (0)47 55042
The Belturbet Festival of the Erne, a 10-day festival is held in July/August, with events and activities to suit all ages. It incorporates the Lady of the Erne pageant, a town talent competition, fancy dress, parades and live music.

Other activities in Belturbet include golf and horse riding, with the Redhills Equestrian Centre providing four-star accommodation, specialist children's holidays, walks and bicycle hire. Belturbet Golf Club is a nine-hole, par 68 course with the majority of holes played to elevated greens.

### 6. Cruising
Public mooring areas are available in Belturbet and a major marina in the town provides for cruisers of all sizes. Cruisers can be hired locally and two-hour cruises on the River Erne are also available (see p149).

Enjoying the music at the Belturbet Festival

## Fishing

### 7. International Fishing Centre
**T:** 00353 (0)49 9522616

### 8. Belturbet Course Angling Association
**T:** 00353 (0)49 9524074

### 9. Belturbet Row Boat Club and Tackle Shop
**T:** 00353 (0)49 9522400
The International Fishing Centre is a specialist anglers' facility in Belturbet providing cottage accommodation, angling organisation and consultancy, as well as boat hire, tackle and bait. It also has its own fishing stands and tennis courts on site. The many lakes, streams and rivers in the Belturbet area provide excellent pike, coarse, and game fishing. Fishing festivals are held throughout the year. Other local providers sell tackle and bait, organise festivals and hire boats (see p147).

The bountiful autumn harvest gathered from Crom Estate

The River Erne at Belturbet

# Ballyconnell

Ballyconnell was founded on land granted to Captain Culme and Walter Talbot during the Plantation of Ulster. In 1619 the town had a three-storey castle surrounded by a defensive wall. Ballyconnell House, still standing across the river from the main street, was built on the site in 1764.

The town lies at the foot of Slieve Rushen, the south-eastern boundary of Bréifne. Its Gaelic name is *Béal Átha Conaill* (Conall's Ford-approach), referring to the legendary warrior of the Red Branch Knights of Ulster, Conall Cearnach. The town has two principal thoroughfares, the main street and the Woodford River, which is part of the Shannon-Erne waterway.

Its Gaelic football club, founded in 1885, was the

Traditional shopfronts in Ballyconnell

first in Ulster and is still called the Ballyconnell First Ulsters. Today the town attracts those keen on golfing, walking, fishing, and cruising. There are several pubs, restaurants and a nightclub, and festivals are held every summer usually in July.

Ballyconnell is located 28km from Cavan town, 31km from Enniskillen and 93km from Sligo.

## Accommodation and eating out

Ballyconnell offers superb accommodation with the four-star Slieve Russell Hotel and Country Club located on the outskirts of the town. There are also good country house, holiday home, and B&B options.

The Connall Cearnach restaurant in the Slieve Russell offers fine dining,

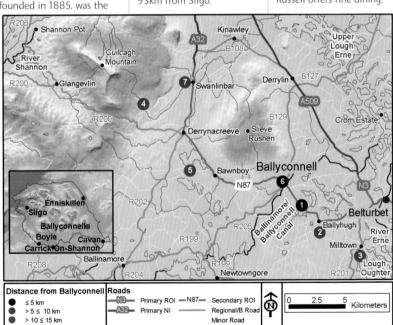

## 1. Slieve Russell Hotel and Country Club

The Slieve Russell Hotel in Ballyconnell

The hotel offers top class accommodation, dining and activities

**T:** 00353 (0)49 9526444   **W:** quinnhotels.com

.Set on 300 acres, including 50 acres of lakes, the four-star Slieve Russell Hotel and Country Club is one of the finest hotels in Ireland's north-west. It has a championship golf course, leisure and health centre, two bars and three restaurants. The 18-hole golf course is in the top 20 inland courses in Ireland and is sensitively wrapped around the lakes and drumlins of the Cavan landscape. Clubhouse facilities include the Summit Bar and Restaurant, and there are magnificent panoramic views over the golf course, which has become one of the top ranking in Ireland. There is pro shop, a nine-hole, par-three course and floodlit driving range.

Leisure facilities at the hotel include a 20m pool, jacuzzi, steam room, sauna and fitness suite and there are extensive conferencing facilities. The latest beauty and holistic treatments from all over the world are also available at the Ciúin Spa and Wellness Centre.

while the Setanta Restaurant offers a more informal setting. Other restaurants include the Anglers Rest, serving pub food all day and dinner in the evenings, and The Quays Italian Restaurant. On the main street is the highly acclaimed cottage style Polo D Restaurant. Owner-chef Paul O'Dowd has received excellent reviews from food critics.

### Information point

**Cavan Tourist Office**

Farnham Street, Cavan
**T:** 00353 (0)49 4331942
**W:** cavantourism.com
**Open:** Seasonal

### 1. Slieve Russell Wedge Tomb

At the Slieve Russell Hotel there is a fine example of a wedge tomb, a type of monument built in the period 2700 BC to 1700 BC (see p73). The tomb

has a long gallery within a low round cairn. Excavations have uncovered bones, some of which were burnt, Early Bronze Age pottery, and small stone-lined boxes.

### 2. Ballyhugh Arts and Cultural Centre

**T:** 00353 (0)49 9526044

Located five minutes' drive from the Slieve Russell Hotel, Ballyhugh Arts and Cultural Centre houses exhibitions and runs courses and

The world famous fiddle player, Martin Hayes, tunes up with Dennis Cahill, before appearing at the Ballyhugh Arts and Cultural Centre

workshops in arts, traditional crafts, Irish music, creative writing and dance. Live shows, traditional concerts and ceilis are held year round. The centre houses a unique

### Conall Cearnach

Conall Cearnach, a legendary Gaelic chieftain and warrior lived at Rathcroaghan, Co Roscommon, the ancient capital of Connaught and the site of the palace of Queen Maeve. Maeve persuaded Conall to murder her husband, Ailill, because she had become jealous of an affair he was having with one of her servants. Conall did so with a cast of his javelin. Ailill's followers then pursued Conall as far as Ballyconnell, where he was eventually slain and beheaded. His head was retained at Rathcroaghan and it apparently gave extra strength to those who drank from the skull.

The Iron Age Stone Idol, believed to represent Conall Cearnach, in Armagh Cathedral

Image ©Rob Vance

collection of artefacts and local heritage photographs. Details of events are published weekly in the local papers or on www.cavantourism.com.

### 3. Drumlane monastic site
🔲🅿 Sitting between Drumlane and Derrybrick loughs are the remains of a sixth-century monastery founded by St Mogue, the Bishop of Ferns. A round tower standing over 11m high is one of the most striking features of the site. Carvings of birds adorn the

©Office of Public Works

An interesting feature of the monastery are the stone heads

The sixth-century Drumlane monastic site    ©Office of Public Works

external wall. The church features a number of interesting stone heads, one above the door in the west wall and another three on the external face of the east window. Near the church, some 150m south, is a series of earthworks, probably the remains of a twelfth-century Augustinian priory which may have been demolished in the fifteenth and sixteenth centuries.

### 4. Tullydermot Falls
❇ The dramatic waterfalls are situated approximately 6km south-west of Swanlinbar in the direction of the Bellavally Gap. The Tullydermot viewpoint overlooks Slieve Rushen and the lowlands of north Cavan. There is also a good view of the summit of Cuilcagh Mountain. The falls are a short distance from the lay-by.

The fast flowing waters of Tullydermot Falls

## The O'Reillys

Still a common name in Bréifne, the O'Reillys (Ó Raghailligh) descended from the Ui Briuin, a tribe that inhabited the central area of Connaught during the fifth and sixth centuries.

In the eighth century part of this kin-group broke away and entered Bréifne, to become known as the Ui Briuin Bréifne. In turn, this group divided again into Muintir Maelmordha (the people of Maelmordha), and the O'Rourkes. In the ninth and tenth centuries many families in Ireland did not have surnames and the Muintir Maelmordha only assumed the surname O'Reilly in the eleventh century. The name is believed to have originated from a member of their family called Raghallach.

The O'Reillys first challenged the O'Rourke leadership of the kingdom of Bréifne in the 1150s, but it was only in the following century

that they really began to threaten the O'Rourke authority. By 1239 the O'Reilly lordship extended westward across Bréifne to the sea, although by 1256 the O'Rourkes had been restored to at least part of their lands. The division of Bréifne into east and west Bréifne was now permanent.

The O'Reillys allied themselves with the O'Neills of Ulster and in the late sixteenth and early seventeenth century became involved in the Nine Years War, which challenged the authority of the English Crown in Ireland. When six counties were set aside for plantation in 1610, east Bréifne, or Cavan, was included. The O'Reillys were largely dispossessed by the English Crown during this plantation of the area and lost their position as the dominant family in the area.

The O'Reilly family crest.

**5. Bear Essentials**
**T:** 00353 (0)49 9523461
**W:** irishbears.com

🔒♿🚶CC☺ The Bear Essentials workshop and showroom in Bawnboy hand-makes teddy bears. Adults and children can participate in workshops to create a personalised bear, or watch as a teddy is created. Residential workshops are available.

## Walking and cycling

### 6. Wildflower Cycling Holidays
**T:** 00353 (0)49 9523923
**W:** wildflowercycling holidays.com

🚶❄🅿 Personalised cycling breaks covering one day tours, short breaks and family holidays can be arranged. All luggage is transferred betweem accommodation stops and bicycles can be provided.

### 7. Cuilcagh Mountain Hostel
**T:** 00353 (0)49 9521656
Part of Cuilcagh Mountain has been designated a UNESCO Geopark, an area of outstanding natural beauty and geologic importance. Visitors can explore the limestone caves, lakes, and wildlife of this beautiful natural resource on foot or by bicycle hired locally (see p155). Wildflower Mountain Biking and Cycle Holiday Tours organises cycling tours and itineraries for exploring the west Cavan area, while experienced mountain guides are available at Cuilcagh Mountain Hostel and can provide walks, fishing, pony trekking and mountain biking by arrangement.

Mountain-biking in the uplands of west Cavan

Shooting for teal, mallard and wigeon along the waterways in Cavan

**Bréifne is Ireland's premier location for caving like here at Peter Bryant's Bullock Hole on Cuilcagh Mountain**

# THE BRÉIFNE LANDSCAPE

Travellers through the north-west of Ireland cannot fail to notice the dramatic change in landscape on entering the Bréifne region. Gone are the mountains of Donegal and the low-lying fields of Connaught and Leinster. Instead one encounters a landscape of gentle, flat-topped hills separating wide lush valleys.

The thin beds of limestone at Streedagh Point were deposited in a tropical sea over 300 million years ago

The Whale Rock glacial erratic in Marble Arch Caves European Geopark

The tale of the formation of the landscape is one of lost oceans, tropical coral reefs, collisions of continents and kilometre-thick sheets of ice – all bound up with Ireland's journey around the globe. Around 330 million years ago, Ireland lay close to the equator and was covered by a warm, tropical sea. The climate was very much like that of the Bahamas today, and the sea was filled with exotic life forms such as coral reefs. It wasn't just the climate that was different back then. During this period of time, known to geologists as the Carboniferous (360-290

million years ago), the Earth spun faster on its axis and there were around 380 days in each year.

Geology is central to understanding how the Bréifne landscapes developed. The story of how the spectacular vistas took shape is written everywhere in the rocks. They formed the ancient cairns and tombs that dot the landscape. They sometimes provided weaponry, and were used to build mighty abbeys and castles, as well as field boundaries, sweathouses and holy wells.

The amazing effects of rainwater on the porous limestone in parts of Bréifne has created an underground world

## Streedagh fossils

A sequence of limestone rocks on the Sligo coast at Streedagh Point provides evidence of the tropical climate Bréifne once enjoyed. Westwards from the beach, around the headland, the rocks contain fossils of many different types of animals that once lived in the shallow sea that covered this area 330 million years ago. As the marine animals died their remains accumulated on the sea floor, became buried in lime-rich mud and became fossilised. The rocks include fossils of shelled animals such as crinoids (sea lilies) and huge corals. This is an important geological heritage site and collection of fossil material is strictly prohibited. Please do not hammer the rocks or fossils.

**Evidence that Ireland once lay close to the equator can be seen in the remains of warm water fossils at Streedagh Point**

Rocks form part of the local folkore traditions and link to the present by providing the material for modern homes and roadways.

Bréifne's geology reveals the immense timeframe it took to create this beautiful and unique landscape in Ireland's north-west. Modern-day activities are now enjoyed on these landscapes that are millions of years old. The steep-sided, table-top mountain ranges, beaches, waterways and drumlins provide a dramatic setting for all kinds of outdoor pursuits, and these activities form another reminder of the central importance of landscape in the daily lives of the people of Bréifne through the millennia.

### Ancient stones

The form and composition of the twisted gneiss (pronounced 'nice') rocks in Bréifne are a testament to their dramatic journey across the face of the Earth.

For example, the northerly extension of the Ox Mountains, which runs in a very thin strip north-eastwards from Collooney to Manorhamilton, includes some of the oldest rocks in Ireland, in some parts up to 750 million years old. Characterised by a rugged, rounded appearance typical of upland areas further west and north-west, these hills are in stark contrast to the classic 'table-top' Bréifne mountain scenery. Gneiss and granite are

## Stalagmites and stalactites

among the hardest rocks in Bréifne. This hardness means that even today, as much as 1,700 million years after parts of them were first formed, the ancient rocks still stand out among the younger rocks and landscapes that surround them. Good places to see the rock formations are around the southern shores of Lough Gill, on the slopes of Slieve Deane near Ballysadare, or along walking routes in Union Wood near Collooney.

### A cave haven

Over the last 10-20,000 years, as the land continued to evolve, large cave systems developed deep within the limestone rocks that lie under much of Bréifne, making this area Ireland's premier location for caving.

Limestone is one of the fundamental aspects of the Bréifne landscape. The

limestone here is often very pure, that is, it is composed almost entirely of the fragmented remains of shelled animals. In marked contrast to the hard ancient gneiss that has resisted the agents of weathering for eons of time, the limestone has a property that is unique within the rocks of the area – it can be dissolved by ordinary rainwater.

When rain falls on limestone it dissolves a tiny part of it. Over thousands of years, this process, called karstification, gradually causes small cracks to open

The best place to see these rock formations is at Marble Arch Caves near Blacklion and Belcoo. Stalagmites and stalactites form as rain water passes down through limestone. The rain slowly dissolves the rock and picks up microscopic amounts of the mineral calcite as it passes. Once the water reaches a gap or break in the rock, such as a cave, the water drips down from the roof of the cave onto the floor below. As it falls it leaves behind a minute amount of calcite on the roof of the cave. Over thousands of years, the small drops of calcite accumulate to form a stalactite. As drops of water hit the floor of the cave, here too a small amount of calcite is deposited, eventually building up a stalagmite. Sometimes stalactites and stalagmites can join to form pillars.

**The Ox Mountains, the oldest in Bréifne, provide the background for Drumcondra Tower House and Bawn**

## The Miners of Arigna

Seamus Lehany

The miners in the Arigna Valley extracted coal from the hillside for over 200 years and many men gave their whole working lives to the task. The memories of the conditions and heavy work are still vivid to men such as Seamus Lehany.

Seamus, who started work in the mines in 1965 at 14 years of age, began on the day shift, hauling the hutches (coal wagons) into the coal face and out again to be winched to the surface. This was the job most new employees started their mining career with. The undulating tunnels were only 1.2m high. A 'back' shift (4.00pm to 12.00am) was responsible for driving the tunnels and blasting. Each team would drive in about one metre per shift and

once this was done, the miners commenced work at the seam.

Only experienced miners worked the coal face because they had to know how to put up the timbers to prevent the roof collapsing. The coal was mined using mechanical hammers and, because the seam was only 30 or 40cm thick, men had to lie on their sides amid the dust that the hammer produced. Carbide lamps were used until the 1970s and these provided seven or eight

metres of visibility but had to be refilled every couple of hours.

One of the worst things that could happen was when miners walked into the invisible 'black damp' (poorly ventilated parts of the mine where carbon dioxide and nitrogen accumulated). Miners who experienced this simply collapsed and had to be carried outside. They were laid on the ground until they revived.

Seamus spent 25 years working at Arigna and a detailed and authentic representation of his and his colleagues' time in the mines can be relived at the Arigna Mining Experience (see p64).

up. As more water passes into the rock, it widens the crack. Eventually large passageways open up and whole rivers can disappear into the limestone and flow underground where they can carve out great cave passages. At the Marble Arch Caves European Geopark near Belcoo and Blacklion, three rivers disappear into the limestone and meet underground as the Cladagh River. Together these underground rivers have created Ireland's most famous caves.

At ground level, where the rock is exposed to the elements, the limestone forms limestone pavement, another distinctive part of the Bréifne landscape. Limestone pavement is an area of bare limestone rock broken up by deep cracks called grykes. Some of the main places in Ireland where limestone pavement can be seen are in Bréifne: the

Limestone pavement on Cuilcagh Mountain

Marlbank National Nature Reserve area, Cuilcagh Mountain and the Burren Forest high above the village of Blacklion. The Burren, here, as in Co Clare, takes its name from *an bhoirin* meaning 'stony place'. The Cavan Way walking route goes through the forest, which also contains the remains of several important archaeological monuments.

## The landscape and industry

In the 1850s, John Caldwell Bloomfield discovered that his newly inherited land around Belleek possessed all the raw materials – feldspar, kaolin, flint, clay and shale – needed for the making of pottery. It was the beginnings of Belleek Pottery, the now famous Parian china product that graces homes and palaces all over the world (see p92). Although local natural resources are no longer used in the pottery, a few kilometres north-west of Belleek on the Ulster Way walking route it is still possible to see the quarry where some of the original feldspar and kaolin was obtained.

In some places in Bréifne the ground is rich in other natural resources, including coal, iron ore and limestone. The area around Lough Allen, for example, has a history of iron production that dates back over 400 years. Sir Charles Coote, a major landowner in the 1600s, originally brought in English and Dutch miners to exploit the iron deposits, establishing a smelter at Creevelea. Belief in the apparently inexhaustible supply and the quality of

Glazing china in Belleek Pottery during the nineteenth century

the iron ore underpinned several other attempts to exploit Bréifne's iron deposits. These had varying degrees of success. The rapid disappearance of forests in Ireland, which were being cleared to make way for agriculture, fluctuations in iron's market price, smelter mismanagement and transport problems all eventually conspired against the industry's success and production finally ceased in 1872.

A blast furnace from the nineteenth century still stands as a reminder of the iron smelter that once stood at Creevelea, and it is said that the Creevelea Ironworks produced the iron for the Halfpenny Bridge in Dublin and Scotland's Tay Bridge.

During the Carboniferous period Bréifne became colonised by great equatorial forests, typically made up of giant tree-like ferns and related plants. As they died and rotted, the plants' accumulated remains became buried and transformed at first into peat and eventually into coal.

There is a long and proud tradition of mining this coal at Arigna. Coal mining first began there in the eighteenth century and continued until 1990. Many families in the surrounding area were dependent on income from employment at the mine, which had some of the narrowest coal seams in the Western world. The history and heritage of mining in Bréifne is presented at the award-winning Arigna Mining Experience Centre (see p65).

The glacial valley at Glencar

## Ice Age influence

It was the Ice Age, however, that had the most significant impact on fashioning the Bréifne landscape we see today. The ice cut down into the gneisses, limestones, mudstones and sandstones,

## The stonemason

Throughout Bréifne there are well over 2,500 archaeological sites where stone has been used to mark ancient burial and ritual sites.

The craft of the stonemason can be traced back to monuments predating the pyramids, through to the Latin inscriptions on Ogham stones between the fourth and eighth centuries, and right up to the construction of stone field boundaries during the Famine times. Close to the Slieve Russell Hotel lies the Ballyhugh Arts and Cultural Centre, and here you can enjoy the work of Joe Bradley, a modern

day craftsman who uses materials which, depending on the stone choice, can be over 700 million years old. Just like the stone, the tools of Joe's trade have hardly changed down the millennia. Lump, walling and sledge hammers; line and straight edge; plugs and feathers to split the stone – all basic tools, and through the skill of the craftsman they transform stone into one of the iconic and enduring images of Ireland's western seaboard.

The most frequently used stones are limestone, granite and sandstone and each carries its own special characteristics. Limestone can shatter easily, granite is more easily shaped and sandstone offers an ever-changing hue.

There is no foundation, yet the dry stone wall offers a solid boundary, a great refuge and haven for Bréifne's abundant wildlife and a strong enclosure for farm animals.

The tools of the stonemason

The stones are millions of years old while the walls themselves are relatively recent additions to the landscape of Bréifne. Like the stones, the skills of the stonemason have come down through the generations. Joe Bradley's work brings it all together – an ancient skill and material still used today at Ballyhugh Arts and Cultural Centre (see page 29) and visible throughout the landscape of Bréifne.

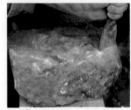
Transforming ancient stone into a a field boundary

widening and deepening valleys. It shaped the rock and debris into smaller drumlins, or hills, and contributed to the formation of many of the region's lakes such as Lough Melvin, Lough Allen, and the spectacular drumlin-filled Lower and Upper Lough Erne. Further evidence of the path the ice took can be seen in places such as the valleys of the Sillees and Arney rivers, which are filled with small elongated, rounded hills all aligned in a similar direction. Elsewhere in Bréifne there are many examples of the valleys the glaciers left behind with Glencar probably being the most spectacular.

## Cursing and praying stones

©Office of Public Works

**Stones like these on Inishmurray Island have a folklore tradition associated with them**

Certain stones in Bréifne are associated with holy wells or early ecclesiastical sites. Usually egg-shaped, cursing and praying stones are often steeped in local folklore and shrouded in mystery. It is believed their use may have pre-Christian origins and that the locations of some Early Christian monasteries were influenced by the proximity of these unusual stones.

The most famous of the cursing stones in Bréifne are the *Clocha Breaca* (Speckled Stones) on Inishmurray Island (see p123).

Over a period of two million years the ice advanced and retreated through Bréifne many times with the last retreat finishing a mere 13,000 years ago. As the ice wasted away, meltwater draining the shrinking ice sheets carried with it the boulders, stones, gravel and sand which had become entombed in the ice depositing them as moraines. During this last advance the ice moved in a general northwestwards direction from the Slieve Anerien-Cuilcagh area and pushed out over the frozen North Atlantic Ocean.

Yet, as would be expected, the Bréifne landscape did not remain static at the close of the Ice Age. After the ice melted a tundra-like landscape was left behind.

Vegetation once again colonised the ice-scoured land and forests of oak, hazel and elm developed. However, climate deterioration, coupled with the actions of Ireland's first farmers, who cleared the land for crops, resulted in large areas of forests being replaced by the now characteristic bog land. In turn the bogs were later extensively drained to make better farmland.

The story of the great landscape carved out by the Ice Age is far from over.

Traditionally they are turned anti-clockwise nine times as certain prayers are said in a 'pattern'. It is believed that the last time these stones were used was to curse Adolf Hitler for causing World War II and the rationing of foodstuffs. Other cursing stone sites include St Brigid's Stones near

## Glacial deposit

**The glacial erratic in the Burren Forest, one of many to be found there**

This huge sandstone boulder pictured in the Burren Forest is known as a 'glacial erratic'. As glaciers move, the advancing ice picks up everything from huge stones to tiny pebbles and can carry them for hundreds of kilometres. The boulder was carried from the top of Cuilcagh Mountain during the last Ice Age. The small rock upon which it sits is limestone. It did not erode due to the protection offered by the boulder. Folklore offers another perspective. Ancient stories tell of the battles between giants who hurled these great boulders at each other...

Bréifne will continue to change and evolve in a timeframe so slow it is difficult to imagine. The rock formations have taken millions of years to form and yet there is more of the story to come.

Killinagh Church, outside Blacklion. By contrast the stones at Toomour near Ballymote, and Killerry, near Dromahair are holy or curing stones. They look the same as cursing stones, but when turned clockwise they become holy, praying or curing stones.

The path of the ice can clearly be seen at Carrowkeel

# BOYLE – CARRICK-ON-SHANNON – DRUMSHANBO

## Boyle

Boyle was founded at the end of the sixteenth century, although there has been a settlement there since the Early Medieval period. Strategically positioned on the edge of the Curlew Mountains, the town was important to the English who were attempting to conquer Connaught, and between 1595 and 1603 the town became an increasingly important military base. It was granted to Joseph Bingley and Joseph King in 1603 and incorporated as a borough in 1613.

Situated at a ford on the River Boyle, a tributary of the Shannon, the town is close to the beautiful Lough Key. Boyle's Gaelic name *Mainistir na Búille* (Monastery of the River Boyle) is a reference to the Cistercian monastery on the shores of the river. To the north and east are the lowlands of Lough Arrow and Lough Key, while to the north-west rise the Bricklieve and Curlew Mountains.

Boyle lies close to the Curlew Mountains

Boyle is an area of immense historical and archaeological interest and a major centre for river and lake fishing. The annual arts festival, which takes place mainly in the fine setting of King House, has an international reputation. Tourist attractions such as the twelfth-century abbey, the Lough Key amenity and beautiful walking trails make the town a popular destination in Bréifne. A weekly farmers market for organic food

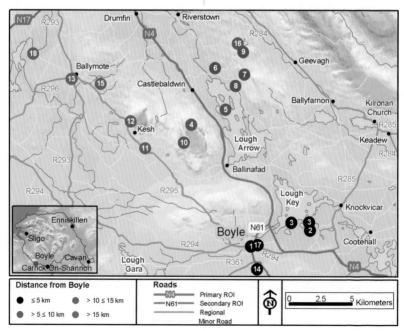

products also attracts both locals and visitors.

Boyle is on the N4 from Dublin. From Belfast take the M1, then follow the A4 to Enniskillen and from there the N16 to Sligo. From Sligo take the N4 to Boyle.

## Accommodation and eating out

Accommodation includes the Royal Hotel on Bridge Street, and a range of guesthouses, B&Bs, self-catering cottages and caravan and camping sites. Places to eat out include Chambers,' Clarke's and Malangies Restaurants in the town centre, Bruno's Italian Restaurant and The Moorings in nearby Knockvicar, Cromleach Lodge in Ballindoon and Clevery Mill in Castlebaldwin. Pub grub is widely available and there is a good selection of cafés.

## Information points

### 1. Ireland West Tourist Office
King House
T: 00353 (0)71 9662145
W: irelandwest.ie
Open: May–September

### Úna Bhán Tourist Co-operative
King House
T: 00353 (0)71 9663033
W: unabhan.net
Open: All year

### King House
T: 00353 (0)71 9663243
W: kinghouse.ie
Open: April–September

This magnificently restored Georgian townhouse was built between 1720 and 1740 for Sir Henry King,

## 17. Boyle Abbey

The Abbey gave the town its Gaelic name, Mainistir na Búille

Images ©Office of Public Works
**Open:** April-October. T: 00353 (0)71 9662604

Regarded as the finest of the Cistercian churches to survive in Ireland, the well preserved Boyle Abbey was founded around 1161. The church was not consecrated until some time between 1218 and 1220, almost 60 years after the first stones were laid. This was the result of scant resources and war. The abbey's turbulent history after it was completed saw it plundered many times in feuds between the local ruling families and occupied and suppressed by the English. From 1599 until the end of the eighteenth century it was used as a military garrison and known as Boyle Castle. It was also besieged in 1645 during the Cromwellian wars.

The abbey has a conventional cruciform plan with a nave and aisles, a transept with four chapels and a square chance. The stone carvings of people and animals on the tops of the pillars are not found in Cistercian abbeys in other parts of Europe or even in other parts of Ireland. Although all the abbots were Gaelic, it appears the influence of an English master-mason is reflected in

the architectural features of the building. The abbey reflects the change of styles, from Romanesque to Gothic, occurring at the time of construction.

Artefacts and other information resulting from excavations of this important site are exhibited in a museum inside Boyle Abbey.

The stone carvings are unique to Boyle Abbey

whose family were one of the wealthiest and most powerful in Ireland. The fine reception gallery, original stone floor, tripartite windows and high vaulted ceilings are all suggestive of its stately home status. After its first life as a home, King House became a military barracks to the famous Connaught Rangers (see p47). The house contains a range of exhibitions on the area's heritage and culture

and can be enjoyed by all ages. There is a restaurant in the grounds, a tourist office, conferencing facilities and guided tours.

The impressive hallway in King House

## Maureen O'Sullivan

**Maureen O' Sullivan as seen with Johhny Weismuller in the Tarzan films**

Maureen O'Sullivan (1911-1998), film actor, was born in Boyle. She trained as an actor in London and Paris and made some 68 films between 1930 and 1988. Her big break came when she was cast to play Jane Parker alongside Johnny Weissmuller in the *Tarzan* series of films. She played Jane six times, and in 1942 largely retired from acting to look after her family of seven children with John Farrow, to whom she remained married until his death. Her other noteworthy films included a role in the Marx Brothers' *A Day at the Races*. When she eventually returned to the big screen she appeared in *Hannah and Her Sisters* (1986) and *Peggy Sue Got Married* (1986). Mia Farrow, star of *Rosemary's Baby* and other notable films, is her daughter. Maureen died in Scotsdale, Arizona in 1998.

## 2. Lough Key Forest Park

❄♿ Consisting of some 860 acres of forest and open parkland, Lough Key Forest Park, is one of Ireland's best lakeside amenity areas. Situated 4km from Boyle, the park combines walks, wildlife, beautiful scenery and lakeside attractions. It was formerly part of the Rockingham Estate. There are approximately 10km of forest walks and trails along

**Autumn bounty of chestnut, acorns and hazelnuts picked in Lough Key Forest Park**

lake shores and forested areas. Boat tours are available, and other amenities include a well landscaped caravan and camping park, nature walks, a bog garden, observation tower, ice house, wishing chair and underground tunnels.

## 3. Islands on Lough Key

🏛❄♿ Castle Island, or the Rock of Lough Key, is dominated by a massive folly in the shape of a castle, built as part of Rockingham Estate in the late eighteenth or early nineteenth century. The folly (an architectural term for an extravagant or fanciful building) was probably a summer residence. The island also contains the remains of a medieval building, probably a MacDermott fortress from the thirteenth century. The island is privately owned and it is best viewed from the shoreline. Trinity Island holds the remains of the Holy Trinity Monastery, founded around the year

1215. *The Annals of Loch Cé*, a chronicle of local and Irish affairs from 1014 to 1570, were compiled in this monastery. A church and one part of the monastic buildings survive. Also in private ownership, the island is best viewed as part of the boat tour leaving from the harbour at Lough Key Forest Park.

The islands also hold the story of Uná Bhán, the daughter of a MacDermott chieftain. She fell in love with a neighbour called Tomás Laidir Costello. However, MacDermott would not allow their marriage. Tomás was banished from the area and Uná Bhán was confined on Castle Island. She went into a deep melancholy, died of a broken heart and was buried on Trinity Island. In his grief Tomás swam to the island every night to keep vigil at her grave. Eventually he got pneumonia and, realising that he was dying, requested that MacDermott allow him to be buried beside Uná Bhán. His request was granted and thus the two lovers were belatedly united.

## 4. Carrowkeel

🏛❄♿▶ Carrowkeel, 15km north of Boyle, is a collection of 23 Neolithic passage tombs located at prominent points on the hilltops of the Bricklieve Mountains. They are visible from great distances all around the Bricklieves. These tombs predate the Egyptian pyramids, and the Carrowkeel complex contains what is possibly the largest known Neolithic stone village in Ireland. Most of the tombs are built from limestone and date

## The Connaught Rangers

King House in Boyle is another of the great houses of Bréifne (see p14). Built originally as a family home around 1730 by Sir Henry King, it later became a military barracks to the famous Connaught Rangers between the years 1788 and 1922.

The Irish regiment was started by Thomas de Burgh, Earl of Clanricarde, and the Connaught Rangers name reveals that it was predominantly raised from the province of Connaught. The Rangers' badge was the harp and crown, with an elephant and sphinx representing campaigns in India and Egypt. For 130 years the Rangers saw service all around the globe and fought in France and at Gallipoli during World War I.

Reports from Ireland of Black and Tan atrocities in June 1920 precipitated a mutiny among the 1st Battalion stationed in India. Members of the regiment at Jullundur informed their officers that they would no longer obey orders as a protest against the atrocities. Two days later another detachment of the Rangers at Solan followed their example. They were led by Private James Daly originally from Ballymoe, Co Roscommon.

Two of the mutineers died in the attack on the armoury at Solan and 69 men were court-martialled. Fourteen of these were sentenced to death, including Charles Kerrigan from Manorhamilton. His death-sentence notice contained a recommendation for mercy because of his youth. He was 18 years of age and the second youngest in a regiment of 400 men. All the sentences were commuted to life imprisonment, except James Daly's. He was executed by firing squad on 2 November 1920 at Dagshai Prison. In 1970 his remains were returned to Ireland and re-interred in Tyrellspass cemetery. The remaining mutineers were released after the Anglo Irish Treaty and returned to Ireland in 1923. The famous Connaught Rangers were finally disbanded in July 1922.

King House provides an insight into the history of the regiment and has numerous other displays and interactive exhibitions.

The 1st Battalion, Connaught Rangers in India — Images ©King House — Model of Private Daly at King House

from 3800 to 3300 BC. The remains of the extensive village can be seen by going to the edge of the ridge (the exit from the complex is the same route as you entered and not down the eastern side of the mountains). There are spectacular views of Co Sligo from the top of the Bricklieve Mountains and the entire area is rich in archaeological features.

The Carrowkeel tomb complex sits on top of the Bricklieves

The bluebell extravaganza in the woods around Lough Key

## Turlough Carolan

Carolan was one of Ireland's greatest harpists and composers. Born in Co Meath, he spent most of his life travelling in Ulster and Connaught. His family lived in Ballyfarnon from around 1684. Blinded by smallpox from around eighteen, he learned to play the harp and entertained many of the great Irish families to whom he dedicated many of his airs. Carolan married Mary Maguire from Fermanagh and lived in Mohill, Co Leitrim. In 1738 he returned to Alderford, the home of his patron Madam MacDermott Roe, where he died. He was buried in Kilronan churchyard, between Keadue and Ballyfarnon, after a wake lasting four days. Huge crowds from around Ireland attended. The Carolan Harp Festival and Summer School takes place each year in Keadue during late July and early August.

Heapstown Cairn.

### 5. Lough Arrow

Lough Arrow is an important over-wintering site for many species of waterfowl and in summer it is a breeding ground for great crested grebe and the common scoter, an extremely rare bird in Ireland. Important habitats such as alluvial woodland and wetlands are also present. The Lough is renowned for the quality of its brown trout and it was here, in the early 1900s, that the technique of spent knat-fishing with dry flies was pioneered. It is situated approximately 30km from Sligo, 10km from Boyle and close to Castlebaldwin.

### 6. Heapstown Cairn

The largest cairn in Ireland outside the Boyne Valley, Heapstown Cairn has not been excavated but is thought to be a passage tomb associated with the Carrowkeel complex (see p46). It probably dates from the Neolithic period, around 3000 BC, and is 60m in diameter with a kerb of large slabs. The cairn is referred to in many legends, such as the Battle of Moytura, and is also reputed to be the burial place of Ailill, a brother of Niall of the Nine Hostages.

### 7. The Labby Rock

The Labby Rock is a massive portal tomb (see p73), with a 60-tonne limestone cap built during the Neolithic period (4000-2500 BC). It has not been excavated in modern times and most likely contains a single burial chamber. It is called labby after *leaba*, the Gaelic word for bed and this name has its origin in the folk belief that Diarmuid and Gráinne slept there when fleeing from Fionn MacCumhaill. Folklore also says it is the burial place of Nuada of the Silver Arm, a king of the Tuatha de Danann. The two portal stones at the front have a blocking stone behind them to seal the chamber.

### 8. Ballindoon Priory

Ballindoon Priory overlooks Lough Arrow and was founded in

Lough Arrow

**The Labby Rock with its huge capstone**

1507 by Thomas O'Farrell and built under the patronage of John MacDonagh, the local Gaelic-Irish lord. It is Gothic in style and has an unusual triple vaulted archway, which would have divided the church into the nave and chancel. Despite the difficulties of persecution the Dominican friars remained in the locality for centuries. The abbey was granted to the King family in 1660. A bullaun stone (which is a hollowed out stone basin) called St Dominic's Stone usually contains water said to cure warts and is located 50m north-east of the priory beside a hawthorn bush.

## Brigadier General Michael Corcoran

Brigadier General Michael Corcoran, Young Irelander and patriot, was born in Carrrowkeel in 1827 and commanded the famous Fighting 69th Irish Regiment in the American Civil War. The Regiment fought gallantly at the Battle of Bull Run and Corcoran was injured and captured by the Confederate Army. Upon his release he moved to New York but died tragically as a result of a fall from his horse. The Mayor of New York, Michael R Bloomberg, unveiled a statue to Corcoran in Ballymote and presented a sod of turf from Corcoran's grave as a symbolic homecoming gesture.

**Michael R Bloomberg**

### 10. Bricklieve Mountains

The Bricklieves are composed of limestones of the same age and composition as the Dartry limestone found in north Sligo and Fermanagh. They are 'table mountain-type' hills, similar if less dramatic in appearance to the Benbulben-Tievebaun range. The Bricklieves comprise four hills, separated by

Image ©Mike Brown

**The peregrine is one of Ireland's majestic birds of prey. A resident, it favours cliffs like those in the Bricklieves for breeding**

north-south-trending dry valleys that formed as a consequence of dissolution of the limestone along joints or cracks. Walkers and climbers of all descriptions can explore the caves and extensive limestone pavement on the Doonaveeragh-Mullaghfarna plateau at the east side of the mountains. The area is particularly noted for its orchid-rich grasslands and for the presence of the rare small white orchid. You can also glimpse ravens and peregrines flying among the cliffs.

Winter snow covers Ballindoon Priory

### 9. Lough Nasool

✖ Lough Nasool, 5 km north-east of Castlebaldwin (right turn when travelling from Boyle to Castlebaldwin), is the best example in Ireland of a vanishing lake. The limestone bedrock contains a sinkhole at the southern end of the lake (top right). It is usually plugged by glacial clay but under high-water conditions it is forced open and the lake drains completely. There is evidence that Lough Nasool drains underground into Lough Bo, which lies on the other side of the drumlin ridge.

## 11. Toomour Church

The ruins of the twelfth century church at Toomour can be found on the road between Boyle and Ballymote. There is an early medieval *leacht cuimhne*, or low, rectangular dry-stone faced cairn, which may have marked a saint's grave or acted as an outdoor altar. The flat slab in front of the leacht is a saint's stone, with depressions apparently made by the saint's knees. The leacht is known in local tradition as the 'Grave of the Kings', named after a number of chieftains buried here following a battle in 971.

## 12. The Caves of Kesh

The Ballymote to Boyle road is notable for the spectacle of 13 small caves at the foot of a steep limestone cliff. Excavations in the caves have uncovered the bones of many animals, including some now extinct in Ireland: bear, wolf, reindeer and lemming. A Neolithic stone axe was also found, along with human bone and teeth dated to the Iron Age. The caves used to be an important assembly site for a fair and sports day on Garland Sunday, the last Sunday of July. They are best viewed from the roadway.

© **Royal Irish Academy**

The principal scribes on the *Book of Ballymote* were Solam Ó Droma, Robertus Mac Sithigh and Magnus Ó Duibgennain, all of whom were pupils of the great Brehon McEgan

## 13. Ballymote Castle and the Book of Ballymote

This imposing Anglo-Norman castle is almost square in plan and has massive three-quarter round towers at each angle (see p78). The famous manuscript, *The Book of Ballymote*, was compiled here. Written mostly in Gaelic the book contains a key to the Ogham alphabet and includes various genealogical and biblical material. It appears to have belonged to the Mac Donnchaid and was purchased in 1522 by O'Donnell, prince of Tir Conaill. It turned up in Trinity College in 1686 and was reported missing in 1702. It was presented to the Royal Irish Academy in 1785 having allegedly been purchased from a millwright's window in Drogheda for £20.

## Arts and entertainment

Boyle Arts Festival takes place every July and is renowned for the quality and variety of arts and entertainment ranging from exhibitions, jazz, traditional

**Performers at the Boyle Arts Festival**

and world music, drama, literature, storytelling and singers' nights to comedy, workshops and children's programmes.
The local pubs also provide ample opportunity for a good night, or day, out. There is a selection of

## Brother Walfrid

**The memorial to Brother Walfrid Kerins, founder of Glasgow Celtic Football Club, in Ballymote**

Brother Walfrid (1840-1915) is the religious name of Andrew Kerins, a Marist Brother and founder of the famous Glasgow Celtic Football Club in Scotland. Brother Walfrid was born in Ballymote in 1840. He moved to Scotland in 1887 where he founded Celtic as a means of raising funds for the poor and deprived in Glasgow. The choice of Celtic as the team name reflected his Irish roots and was adopted by the club in 1887. In 2005 the club erected a statue in honour of Brother Walfrid outside the main entrance to Celtic Park.

## 18. Irish Raptor Centre and Eagles Flying

entertainment in pubs such as the Moving Stairs, Moylurg Inn, Clarke's, An Crannóg and Patrick's Well. Local musicians come together to play traditional music on Thursday nights in Lavin's pub and on Friday nights in Wynne's pub.

## Fishing

There are some excellent locations for game and coarse fishermen in the area, such as the Boyle River, which runs from Lough Gara through the town and on to Lough Key. Locally, tench to 6lb are common and in Lough Gara, a noted pike fishery, fish to 20lbs are regularly recorded (see p146).

### 14/15. Boyle Golf Club
Located in Knockadoo to the south of the town, off the N61, this is a nine-hole parkland course with full clubhouse facilities. There are two other courses nearby at Carrick-on-Shannon and Ballymote.

### 16. Lough Bo Shooting Centre
**T:** 00353 (0)86 8396620
**Open:** All year
The centre offers clay pigeon shooting in country surroundings and is located just outside Riverstown. All equipment is supplied and there are practice or private tuition sessions available. There is also an all-weather shooting range and group sessions can be organised.

**T:** 00353 (0)71 9189310
**W:** eaglesflying.com

Ireland's biggest sanctuary for birds of prey and owls, is just outside Ballymote. Some of the biggest birds of prey in the world can be observed in their natural environment. The centre runs bird shows twice daily, featuring free-flying eagles, hawks and vultures, and is a great experience for all ages. Valuable information on the habitat needs of these birds is also provided. The free-flying exhibitions, which take place daily at 11am and 3pm, are particularly memorable.

The centre also fulfils an important role as a hospital for injured species and is part of a breeding network for release programmes.

# Carrick-on-Shannon

Carrick-on-Shannon was established in the early seventeenth century as part of the English policy of plantation in Ireland. It was granted a charter in 1613, which established it as an incorporated town, probably because of its strategic location on a crossing of the River Shannon. A newly-built castle was granted to Maurice Griffith in 1611 and he later built a fort and a wooden bridge in the town. During the confederate wars of the 1640s Carrick was held by the Earl of Clanrickard who fought off attacks by Eoghan Roe O'Neill. Its position on the Shannon Waterway meant that it was a major depot for river trade from the nineteenth century onwards. Carrick-on-Shannon, which in Gaelic is *Cora Droma*

Carrick-on-Shannon is a great base to enjoy the Shannon-Erne waterways

*Rúisc* (Weir of the Ridge of the Tree Bark), is the county town of Leitrim. It is situated in a landscape defined by the floodplain of the modern River Shannon, and the ancient paths of glaciers, which left fields of drumlins interspersed with rivers and lakes.

It has a thriving town centre with modern marina facilities, attractive streetscapes and traditional shop fronts.

Situated on the N4, 157km north-west of Dublin and 56km south-east of Sligo, Carrick is a gateway town for Bréifne and the cruising capital of the Shannon.

## Accommodation and eating out

Carrick-on-Shannon accommodation ranges through guesthouses, B&Bs, hostels, self-catering cottages and hotels, which

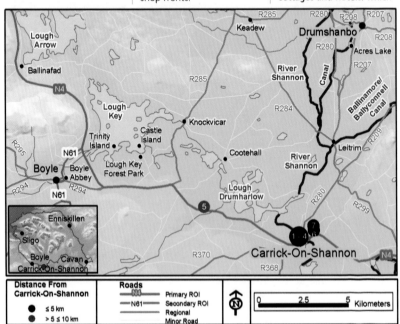

include the four-star Landmark Hotel and the three-star Bush Hotel. There is a great selection of restaurants, as well as fast food, coffee bars, cafés and pubs, many with a nautical theme and riverside culture. The Moon River pleasure-cruiser, which seats 110 passengers, also provides a different experience with full bar service and catering.

Carrick offers plenty of opportunity for fine dining

## Information point

**1. Tourist Information Office**

ℹ️ Old Barrel Store
Carrick-on-Shannon
**T:** 00353 (0)71 9620170
**W:** leitrimtourism.com
**Open:** Seasonal

**2. McCann Memorial Monument**
The town clock, a popular

The Costello Chapel

meeting point, is properly known as the McCann Memorial Monument. It was erected in 1905 in memory of Owen McCann, a prominent citizen and first chairman of Leitrim County Council. When the monument was moved to its present site the clock was restored to working order.

Adjacent to the monument is the Dock Arts Centre where the old courthouse once stood. Following the 1798 defeat of the United Irishmen and the French Army by Cornwallis and Lake at Ballinamuck, a large number of prisoners were

held here. Cornwallis ordered that a lottery be held among the Irish prisoners to establish who would be hanged. Some 17 prisoners were hanged at this spot and the plaque by

## The Dock Arts Centre

The Dock is Leitrim's latest centre for the arts

**T:** 00353 (0)71 9650828
**W:** thedock.ie

♿ CC P 🔒 The Dock is Carrick-on-Shannon's integrated centre for the arts and is housed in the nineteenth-century former courthouse building. Featuring exhibitions, performances, art galleries, studios, classes and workshops, it is housed in the beautifully restored nineteenth century courthouse building, overlooking the Shannon and has a 100+ seat performance space. The Dock also houses Leitrim Design House, where a variety of artisans are located. Knitwear, cutlery, furniture pieces, one-off craft products and clothing are available (see page 166).

The Landmark Hotel

Modern art exhibition at the Dock

## John McGahern

John McGahern (1934-2006) was one of Ireland's leading writers and, though born in Dublin, he grew up in Cootehall and Ballinamore, and was educated in Carrick-on-Shannon. He began his career as a teacher, and his first novel, *The Barracks*, was published in 1963. This took its setting from his own childhood as the son of a Garda Sergeant. His second, *The Dark*, was published in 1965 and told the story of an adolescent boy's experience of family and clerical abuse. It was banned in Ireland and led to McGahern's dismissal from his teaching post. He spent the next ten years abroad and on returning to Mohill, Co Leitrim had a number of novels published. One of his finest works is the Booker Prize-nominated *Amongst Women*, which tells the tale of the final years and recollections of a politically-disillusioned former IRA soldier who dominates his family on a small farm in the west of Ireland. His last non-fiction book, *Memoir*, is the story of his childhood and adolescence in Bréifne. He is buried in Aughawillan church yard in Co Leitrim.

the Dock commemorates those who were executed.

### 3. Costello Chapel
✠ Costello Chapel is believed to be the smallest chapel in Europe and the second smallest in the world. Edward Costello, a local shopkeeper, commissioned it in memory of his wife Mary Josephine Costello after she died in 1877, aged 47. The chapel is roughly 5m long and 3.5m wide. On either side of the aisle is a lead-lined coffin containing the remains of Mr and Mrs Costello.

### 4. The Market Yard
**T:** 00353 (0)71 9650816
🛈 €cc This busy shopping and activity centre was formerly a market house and shambles (meat market) and was erected in 1830. Close examination of the lintels of many of the doors in the market yard reveals faint outlines of the names of

traders of a century ago. The renovated Market Yard Centre now contains a hand-crafted crystal outlet, restaurant, café, nautical shop and a farmers market every Thursday.

### 5. Carrick-on-Shannon Golf Club
This is a recently extended 18-hole, par 70 course located on the N4 between Carrick and Boyle. The original nine holes are set in mature parkland whilst the new holes wind their way through wetland and hillocks featuring great views.

### 6. Aura Leitrim Leisure Centre
**T:** 00353 (0)71 9671771
**W:** leitrim.ie
**Open:** All year
🛗✗❄€🅿🚹 Facilities at the centre include gym, fitness studio, health suite and a five-lane pool with learner and toddler pools.

A jazz session during the Carrick Water Music Festival

The Famine statue at Sligo Harbour

## Major Thomas Heazle Parke

Major Thomas Heazle Parke was a surgeon, adventurer and soldier, (1857-1893). He was the first Irishman to cross Africa, as part of the infamous Henry Morton Stanley expedition to the Congo between 1887 and 1889. Almost 600 of the 800 who started on the journey perished and it was Parke who cured Stanley of his fever. His book *My Personal Experiences in Equatorial Africa* (1891), became a best-seller. Born in Kilmore, near Carrick-on-Shannon, he graduated from the Royal College of Surgeons, Dublin. Parke then entered the British Army and served in Egypt. On returning to England after the Congo expedition in 1890 he was presented with gold medals from the British Medical Association and the Royal British Geographical Society. His travels took a toll on his health and he died at the young age of 36 years. He was returned to Drumsna in Co Leitrim where he now lies. There is a striking monument to Thomas Parke at the entrance gate to the Natural History Museum in Dublin.

## 7. The Great Famine and The Garden of Remembrance

Few events in Irish history had such a social impact as the Great Famine (1845-50). In Bréifne the population of Leitrim, for example, was recorded at 155,000 in 1841 and by 1851 was reduced to 112,000. In Fermanagh the severe impact of the Famine saw the population decline from 156,481 in 1841 to 116,047 in 1851. The population decline in Leitrim and Fermanagh at around 25 per cent was considerably greater than the province of Ulster (15.7 per cent) or than in Ireland as a whole (19.9 per cent). The words workhouse, soup kitchen, starvation, emigration, fever and famine graves all suggest the horror that the Great Hunger inflicted on the population.

The landscape of Bréifne contains many poignant reminders of this suffering. Famine graveyards are common and St Patrick's Hospital in Carrick-on-Shannon, originally built as a workhouse, now has a famine memorial garden. The garden, situated to the rear of the hospital, was originally a disused graveyard in which hundreds of victims of the Famine were buried in unmarked graves. In nearby Strokestown, Co Roscommon, there is a Famine museum where you can learn more about this great social upheaval.

The winter solstice, 21 December, on Castlefore Lake near Keshcarrigan

# Drumshanbo

Drumshanbo can trace its history back to cave dwellings alongside Lough Allen dating from prehistoric times. It has been a central point in the industrial heritage of Bréifne, with the coal mining of the Arigna Valley to the north-west and iron mining at Sliabh Anierin (the Iron Mountain) to the north-east.

Drumshanbo is set amid scenic woodland at the southern point of Lough Allen. Its name, from the Gaelic *Droim Seanbhó* (Ridge of the Old Cow), reputedly has its origin in the shape of certain hills in the vicinity, or may derive from *Droim Seanboth* (Ridge of the Old Huts). The distinctive flat-topped plateaux support large expanses of blanket bog. The town is famous for its

musical traditions and a unique feature is its high street, fronted by a stone wall leading up to Ireland's shortest main street. Drumshanbo is also a prized angling town as it sits beside Lough Allen, a major coarse fishing location in Ireland. The town is also a good base for hill-walking

**Main Street in Drumshanbo**

holidays.
Drumshanbo is easily accessible off the N4 from Carrick-On-Shannon on the R208 and is 170km north-west of Dublin, 45km south-east of Sligo and 186km south-west of Belfast.

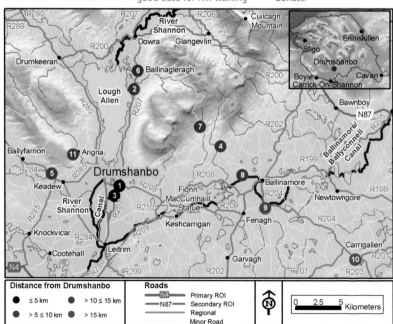

## Accommodation and eating out

The Ramada Hotel complex features many balconies fronting onto Lough Allen. It provides excellent leisure facilities and The Rushes, a top class restaurant. The Moorlands Equestrian Centre is also located within the hotel grounds. Drumshanbo and its hinterland are also served by B&Bs and self-catering chalets. Restaurants, pubs and cafés within the town offer a number of options for eating out.

## Information point

🛈 Tourist Office
Carrick-on-Shannon
Co Leitrim
T: 00353 (0)71 9620170
W: leitrimtourism.com
Open: Seasonal

### 1. 🛈 🅿 Sliabh an Iarainn Visitor Centre
T: 00 353 (0)71 9640678
Open: 9am–5pm
The sights and scenery of Leitrim's lakes, mountains and towns, are told in an audio-visual show at the centre. A number of important features of the area are given special treatment – the mining of coal and iron, sweathouses, and the Cavan and Leitrim Railway. There is also lots of information about what's happening in the area.

### 2. Lough Allen Adventure Centre
T: 00 353 (0)71 9643292
Open: All year
🚣 ❄ This outdoor activity centre is located within easy reach of Drumshanbo on the eastern shores of Lough Allen. It specialises in kayaking, windsurfing and a host of other adventure activities. It caters for all ability levels and also offers safe yet challenging surfing trips to the sea, open boating, rafting, hillwalking, camping expeditions and gorge walks. All necessary equipment can be supplied.

### 3. Acres Lake
Open: All year
🚣 ❄ 🅿 ♿ Acres Lake is situated on the Lough Allen Canal, a thriving pleasure cruising route. This fine jetty-side amenity, just a short walk from the village, has a heated outdoor swimming pool, tennis courts and a children's play area. A teach ceoil (music house) is also located here and hosts Irish music song and dance sessions.

Lough Allen Canal was first constructed in 1818, and ran from Battlebridge to Lough Allen via Acres Lake. Shortly afterwards Ireland entered

A modern statue of Fionn MacCumhaill is located near the village of Keshcarrigan on the Carrick road. Local tradition claims he is buried at a passage tomb at Sheebeg Hill also near the village. The tomb of the legendary leader of the Fianna warriors is located approximately 2km outside Keshcarrigan and off the road to Carrick-on-Shannon. The views at his gorse-covered cairn stretch over Co Leitrim and beyond.

into a period of economic decline and the canal was eventually abandoned in 1900. In 1978 it was restored as far as Acres Lake and by 1996, was fully re-opened into Lough Allen. The remains of the old canal lock can still be seen.

### 4/5. Holy wells
🛖 ✝ There are several holy wells around Drumshanbo, many visited by the devout looking for cures. St Patrick's Well in Aughnasheelan includes a rag tree, a wooden cross, a shrine to St Patrick and two older wells. Opposite Kilronan Church on the road between Ballyfarnon and Keadue is a

Lough Allen has everything for those who enjoy watersports

St Lasair's Well has religious and folkore associations

## John McKenna

John McKenna (1880-1947), an influential and well-known traditional Irish flute player, was born in Tarmon on the western shore of Lough Allen. He worked on the family farm and in the Arigna coal mines before emigrating to America in 1911, where he worked with the New York Fire Patrol. His robust, rhythmic and breathy flute playing is acknowledged as representing the north Leitrim flute playing style. Fellow Irishmen in New York noticed his music skills and he went on to record 30 records between 1921 and 1936. The memorial to him at Tarmon Church, the remains of a late medieval church on the western shore of Lough Allen, was erected in September 1980 to honour his contribution to Irish music and culture.

holy well dedicated to St Lasair. The large flagstone supported by four stones next to the well has a prayer stone on it known as *Leacht Ronain* (Ronan's Altar). Crawling under this three times, and turning the praying stone each time, is meant to be a cure for backache.

### 6/7. Sweathouses
Sweathouses are believed to have been used as saunas. The slopes of Sliabh an Iarainn are dotted with them and good examples can be seen at Ballinagleragh, on the

eastern side of Lough Allen, and Gubnaveagh, on the eastern side of the mountain. Usually beehive-shaped structures with very small doorways, they were traditionally made of stone and turf fires were lit inside to heat the interior. Once it was sufficiently warm, the user remained inside for a while, and then emerged to bathe in a nearby stream. The traditional use was to alleviate rheumatism. While the origins of these sweathouses may be medieval, the examples in Bréifne date from the eighteenth century onwards.

### 8. Ballinamore Golf Club
Located about 20km east of Drumshanbo, Ballinamore is a nine-hole parkland course situated along the Shannon-Erne Waterway. The clubhouse provides bar and snack facilities.

### 9. Glenview Folk Museum
T: 00 353 (0)71 9644157
Near Ballinamore, this museum houses a private collection of over 6,000 antique, historical and novel items from pre-famine Ireland

Sweathouses are common around Sliabh an Iarainn and served the same purpose as modern day saunas

onwards. Included is an impressive array of farmyard equipment, a large selection of tradesman's tools from yester-year and lots of wonderful memorabilia from earlier times.

### 11. Arigna Mining Experien
T: 00 353 (0)71 9646466
W: arignaminingexperience.ie
Open: All year

Located west of Drumshanbo in the hill country of north Roscommon, the Arigna Mining Experience Centre provides a tremendous insight into the world of coal miners and the conditions under which they worked.

The area has a rich mining heritage dating back to the seventeenth century when Charles Coote established iron works at Creevelea and Arigna.

The main coal seam was discovered in 1765 and from then until 1990, coalmining was the main industry in the region.

## Music and festivals

Inaugurated in 1953, Drumshanbo's annual An Tostal Festival in June still presents the finest in Irish music, song, dance and culture. It includes street theatre, concerts, fishing competitions and singing contests. The Joe Mooney Summer School in July draws musicians from all around the globe and during the week-long festival there is lots of music, recitals, lectures and outdoor sessions. There are also annual festivals in Ballinagleragh and Dowra that draw large crowds.

## 10. Corn Mill Theatre

**T**: 00 353 (0)49 4339612
Located in Carrigallen, the theatre has an extensive and varied programme of entertainment from drama (amateur and professional) to variety shows, music and poetry. Check the local press for details of the current programme.

### The MacDermotts

The MacDermott (Mac Diarmada) family descends from Tadhg O'Connor, who was king of Connaught before the Norman invasion. It divided into three groups, the most important being the MacDermotts of Coolavin, formerly of Moylurg, whose territory embraced much of Roscommon. Castle Island on Lough Key was their fortress.

The MacDermott Roe of Alderford are descendants of Dermot Dall (blind Dermot) who was the grandson of Cormac, the King of Moylurg. The MacDermott Gall, the third MacDermott sept (clan), quickly accepted English domination and was all but disregarded in the history of the sept. The fortunes of the MacDermotts of Moylurg went downhill following their involvement in the early seventeenth century rebellion which ended in the defeat of the Irish rebels at the Battle of Kinsale. They lost the last of their lands in the 1660s, but the family name and the title, Prince of Coolavin, continue today.

The MacDermott Roe family did not take part in the Irish rebellion against the English Crown and retained control of their lands. They grew in wealth and power during the eighteenth and nineteenth centuries becoming increasingly anglicised and converting to Protestantism. They became expatriates when Irish nationalism came to the fore.

### Walking

Situated between the Arigna Mountains and Sliabh an Iarainn, Drumshanbo is a good area for hill-walking. There is plenty of choice, from short rambles to day-long hikes. The Leitrim Way, together with the Miner's Way and Arigna Historical Trail, offer waymarked, long-distance walking trails that may be taken as a multi-day hike or piecemeal as single-day walks (see p152).

The coal seams at Arigna were very thin by comparison to those mined in Britain and coalfaces were as low as 30cm, meaning exceedingly cramped conditions for the miners. They had to lie almost flat when working in the cold, damp and watery conditions. The poor quality of three out of the five seams in the area meant the coal was relatively low grade and had high ash content. It primarily supplied heating fuel for local houses, schools and hospitals.

The Arigna Mining Experience looks out across the Arigna Valley and Lough Allen. The underground tour takes about 40 minutes and the guides are all ex-miners. There is an exhibition area, coffee shop and school or group visits can be easily accommodated. It is an experience that cannot be matched anywhere in Ireland.

There is an abundance of great walking trails in the vicinity of Drumshanbo

Standing stones, like this one near Bawnboy in Cavan, date from the Bronze Age making them over 4000 years old

# THE ARCHAEOLOGY OF BRÉIFNE

Bréifne's archaeological sites are among the finest and most well preserved in Ireland. The local landscape is a key element in understanding the rich array of archaeological remains that cover the area's hills, valleys, coastline and plains. These, along with the mountain passes, lakelands and river systems were arteries of trade and exchange, and were also great avenues for the movement of people and ideas for thousands of years.

## The first people

Human settlement began in Bréifne some 9,000 years ago. This was the Mesolithic period, or Stone Age, a time when nomadic and semi-nomadic groups hunted, fished and gathered wild fruits and vegetables. Archaeological evidence suggests Mesolithic people lived in small circular wickerwork huts covered in animal skins. As fish and shellfish were an important part of their diet, the people concentrated near estuaries, lakes or along river systems. Bréifne, like the rest of Ireland, would then have been covered in dense deciduous woodland, with the only open areas being waterways, the coast and the higher mountains.

There have been scattered finds of distinctive stone tools belonging to the later part of the Mesolithic period (c.5500-4000 BC) at the Boyle River, Cushrush Island on Lough MacNean Lower and in the Sillees River near Enniskillen.

## Megalith builders

Megaliths, from the Greek megas lithos (big stone) are the most impressive remnants of the past in Bréifne. The area has around 250 megaliths and 95 cairns, some of international significance. Few places in Ireland have such a concentration of these kinds of monuments.

Construction of the megaliths began around 6,000 years ago, a period known as the Neolithic or New Stone Age. This was the period when the first farmers arrived, and when animals such as cattle and sheep, and plants, such as wheat, arrived in Ireland along with pottery and new types of stone tools. The Bréifne landscape dramatically changed as woodland was cleared to make open fields

for pasture and for cereal growing. The megaliths are remarkable feats of architecture that appear to express the social complexity of the period. Although communal burial practices, mainly cremation, were carried out in these monuments, they also seem to have functioned as places for ritual and religious activity, possibly linked to ancestral worship.

## Bronze Age

About 2500 BC metalworking was introduced into Ireland with the fashioning of copper and gold. By 2200 BC bronze was being used and throughout Bréifne there have been a large number of Bronze Age finds in lakes, bogs and fords. These finds may reflect a ritual of depositing valuable artefacts at watery places, which was possibly an expression of power and prestige. Various types of weapons have also been found in Bréifne, suggesting a society with a developing warrior elite and a growing population.

Although megalithic tombs were still being used at the beginning of the Bronze Age they were later replaced by single cremations and 'inhumations' (the placing of corpses in a crouched position) in simple pits or stone-lined pits called cists. These types of burials are sometimes found in earthen mounds called barrows, as at Rathdooney Beg, 3km north of Ballymote. Stone circles and standing stones are also aspects of this period. Examples can be seen at places like Magh Sleacht near Ballyconnell. Occasionally Neolithic monuments were re-used and some hilltop cairns, such as that on the summit of Cuilcagh Mountain, possibly date from the Bronze Age.

## Carrowmore passage tombs

T: 00353 (0)71 9161534
**Open:** Easter-October

The Carrowmore complex of tombs, 6km west of Sligo City, is one of the greatest megalithic sites in Western Europe. Older than some of the Egyptian pyramids, these monuments form the largest collections of Stone Age structures in Ireland. There may have been as many as 100 monuments built in this area. Today, 84 structures have been identified by archaeological research and 25 definite passage tombs remain. The excavated monuments date to the early part of the Neolithic period, from 4000 BC to 3500 BC. The main concentration of monuments is spread over an area of 600m by 1km and the majority are a mixture of passage tombs and dolmens, usually surrounded by a stone curb and constructed with large rounded boulders. The centrally placed cairn, Tomb 51, appears to occupy the primary location with the others constructed facing it. This is also the only tomb where decoration is evident. Excavations at Tomb 7, which consists of a central chamber surrounded by a boulder circle of 31 boulders, uncovered a large quantity of cremated human bones, together with fragments of antler pins and a stone ball. Quantities of unopened seashells were also found.

## Ringforts, cashels and crannógs

Ringforts are the most common type of historic monument in the Irish landscape today. They are generally fortified circular enclosures defined by an earthen bank and ditch. In areas where soil cover was thin, these defended enclosures were constructed in stone and were called cashels. Crannógs, which are artificial or natural islands in lakes or rivers, were also built up into fortified island dwelling settlements. They have been described as the wetland equivalent of ringforts. Other people would have lived in unenclosed settlements for which there is little evidence on the ground today.

**The Wardhouse, close to Tullaghan, is a good example of a ringfort** Image ©Office of Public Works

## Holy wells

There are some spectacular examples of holy wells in Bréifne, many of which are still actively visited, usually to obtain a cure or blessing for the pilgrim.

The pilgrimage to a well is known as a 'round' or 'pattern' and certain prayers are said in particular order while circling or moving around the well or structures such as trees or bushes associated with it. Articles such as beads, coins or rags are left as tokens for a cure.

Rosary Beads adorn the walls at Ballinagleragh Holy Well

Visiting wells is one of the oldest traditions of Irish Christianity and probably has its roots in pre-Christian ritual. The majority of wells in Bréifne are natural springs and most have been modernised or altered throughout history. The wells are often dedicated to a particular saint, most commonly St Patrick and St Brigid, while others are associated with local saints. The folklore surrounding the wells includes legends of miracles, activities of saints, and a range of cures that can be obtained at each one. Good examples of holy wells can be found at Tobernalt, St Patrick's Wells at Aughnasheelan, Belcoo and Bunduff, St Brigid's Well near Blacklion, St Lasair's Well at Kilronan, Tobar Bheo Aodh at Ballinagleragh and St Mary's Well at Killarga.

Holy well visiting takes place as part of the various rituals and events on festival days, local saints' days, or other important periods in the yearly cycle. The four main festivals are St Brigid's Day (1 Feb), the ancient festival of Imbolc and the beginnings of spring; May Day (1 May), which equates to Bealtine, an ancient fire festival and the beginnings of summer; Garland Sunday or the Lughnasa harvest festival, (normally the last Sunday in July); and, Hallowe'en or Samhain which recorded the beginnings of winter.

Ballinagleragh Holy Well, like many others, was an important religious site

## Iron Age innovation

The arrival of ironworking (c.2,600-1,650 years ago) brought further innovation and social change to Bréifne. Near Boho a wooden cauldron and a spearhead decorated with characteristic La Tene motifs have been found, while the Iron Age Keshcarrigan Bowl was discovered near the village of the same name during construction of the Shannon-Erne canal. Decorated stones and carvings from around Bréifne such as the Killycluggin Stone and the triple headed Corleck Head from near Cavan town also come from this period.

Few definitive Irish Iron Age sites have been excavated but some burial mounds

The Keshcarrigan Bowl dates from the Iron Age and has characteristics also seen on finds in other parts of Europe

known as ring barrows may date from this period. Certain Neolithic megaliths appear to have been re-used as Iron Age burial sites such as that at Carrowmore.

Human teeth found at the Caves of Kesh were dated to the Iron Age. It is possible that promontory forts such as Knocklane, and some hill forts such as Derryragh, near Ballyconnell, or Lisdarush near

Metal spearheads, such as this one from Boho, were made during the Iron Age-over 4000 years after the use of stone axes

Image ©National Museum of Ireland

Manorhamilton date from the Iron Age.

## The Celts

It was once understood that the 'Celts' - tribes of iron-using central European warriors - invaded Ireland and brought iron metalworking technology and other innovations with them. However, it is now believed that no substantial folk movement or so-called 'Celtic' invasion occurred in Ireland. A more likely explanation is that social and technological changes came through trade and interaction between the growing warrior elites along the western Atlantic fringe and that new ideas, new technologies, and even languages were gradually introduced throughout the first millennium BC.

The word Celt was commonly used throughout the nineteenth and twentieth centuries to describe a group of central Europeans who appeared to share similar religious beliefs, social structure and material culture, along with certain linguistic commonalities. They became associated with nineteenth century nationalism. Art styles, such as those found on the Keshcarrigan Bowl, have simiiarities with styles from across Europe. Linguistic similarities

between Irish, Manx, Scots Gaelic, Breton, and Welsh were seen to derive from an ancestral homeland in central Europe. Similarities between gods such as Lugh, along with myths, legends, and the religious practices by the druids witnessed by Classical observers all suggest a common racial origin for the Celts. Certain stories found in Bréifne relating to the Tuatha Dé Danann, Queen Maeve and the adventures of the Fianna may also derive from this Iron Age period.

## Early Christian sites

The beginnings of Christianity in the fifth century marked a new departure in the history of Bréifne. Christian churches were built, sometimes at former pagan sites, and the early Irish church organised itself around a series of monasteries. They were led by abbots or head monks who were the most powerful people in the church.

The Early Medieval monastic sites were typically composed of a circular enclosure (defined by a either a stone wall or earthen bank) which contained a church and a range of monastic buildings including a refectory, a kitchen and monks' quarters. They could also include high crosses, a round tower, cross slabs and a founder's tomb or shrine. Bréifne contains

The Cavan Brooch, from the late eighth or early ninth century

The three faced Corleck Head, found in Cavan, dates from the second century BC. Heads feature prominently in Celtic art

## Four types of megalith

Creevykeel Court Tomb

### Court tomb

The most distinctive feature of a court tomb is a roofless court area from which the main body, or gallery, of the monument was reached. This gallery consists of two or more chambers set behind one another. The chambers had low corbelled roofs and the whole structure would have been covered in a cairn, the edges of which were delimited by large kerbstones or occasional dry-stone walling or both. There are variations on this standard plan that include full, dual, and central court tombs. Aghanaglack court tomb near Boho is a fine example of a dual court tomb. Another good example of a court tomb can be found at Creevykeel.

Image ©National Museum of Ireland

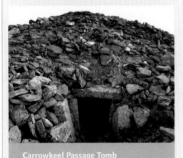

The Calf House Portal Tomb in the Burren Forest

### Portal tomb

Portal tombs, sometimes called dolmens, are often spectacular in appearance due to the impressively sized capstone which covered a single chamber. They are probably the best known of the Irish burial tombs and are generally found in a lowland setting. Most have two tall upright stones (portals) set at the front of the monument so that the capstone rises at the front. Some appear to have been located at the end of a long cairn of stones and in most cases the orientation of the tomb is towards the east. Examples include the Labby Rock near Boyle, and the Lough Scur Dolmen near Keshcarrigan.

Carrowkeel Passage Tomb

### Passage tomb

These generally have a narrow passage leading to a chamber. Smaller chambers sometimes open off the main chamber and occasionally produce a cross shaped or cruciform plan. The roofs were mainly corbelled and the structure was covered in a circular shaped cairn generally edged by kerbstones. Simple passage tombs also occur, comprising a polygonal chamber with a capstone and are often surrounded by a circle of boulders. These simple passage tombs tend to be earlier in date than the more complex ones. Carrowkeel and Carrowmore are sites that provide excellent examples of passage tombs.

### Wedge tomb

The Giant's Leap Wedge Tomb in the Burren Forest

These belong to the late Neolithic (c.2700BC) period and continued to be built into the Bronze Age, up to 1700 BC. They are the most common megalithic tomb in Ireland. They consist of a rectangular main chamber or gallery. Most have a wider entrance often towards the west. A wedge shaped kerb often occurs that was wider at the front and narrower to the rear. Capstones or 'lintels' roofed the chamber and the structure was covered in a cairn. There are some differences from tombs in the Northern and Southern halves of Ireland, possibly reflecting a different period of construction. Examples of wedge tombs in Bréifne include the Giant's Leap in the Burren Forest and one in the grounds of the Slieve Russell Hotel in Ballyconnell.

two of Ireland's finest examples of early monastic sites: Inishmurray Island off the coast at Sligo, and Devenish Island on Lower Lough Erne.

The twelfth century saw the church in Bréifne and the rest of Ireland re-organised to bring it into line with the Catholic Church in the rest of Europe. Ireland was divided into territorial units called dioceses. They were

Image ©National Museum of Ireland

**Named after St Molaise, who founded the monastery at Devenish, the Soiscéal Molaise dates from the early eleventh century and is the oldest surviving book shrine**

controlled by bishops who had full administrative and pastoral authority. This process of church reform also led to the introduction of new monastic orders from the continent, the most important being the Cistercians, whose foundations included Boyle Abbey, and the Augustinians, who established St Mary's Priory on Devenish Island.

Monasteries founded in Bréifne after the reform had a different layout to the early monastic centres. They were built around a square or cloister, with the church building on one side and the other monastic buildings arranged around the other three sides of the square. Boyle Abbey is a well preserved example of this new layout, but here the

monks decorated the monastery in a style unique to western Ireland. Monasteries were usually patronised or funded by local lords, some of whom are commemorated with elaborate tombs. The O'Conor and O'Crean tombs in Sligo Abbey indicate the wealth and power of these patrons.

Twelfth century church reform also meant the introduction of the parish church, still a common feature of the Bréifne landscape. Some were built on sites of former monastic centres. For example, the church at Killery, near Dromahair, while possibly on the site of an early monastic centre, was a parish church some time after the twelfth century.

### Devenish Island

**T:** 00 44 (0)28 9054 6518
**W:** ehnsi.gov.uk
**Open:** April-September

Many people are drawn to explore the early medieval monastic site at Devenish Island (*Daimhinis*, meaning

'Ox Island'), which reflects the importance of this area before the development of Enniskillen town. The monastery was founded by St Molaise in the sixth century and the remains of a number of different building phases can still be seen. These include a series of low earthworks from the

## The Vikings

The first definitive Viking attack on Ireland happened in Bréifne. The initial port of call for the Viking invaders was the monastic settlement on the island of Inishmurray (see p123), which was plundered in 795).

Off the coast of north Sligo, Inishmurray is home to one of the best preserved early Irish monasteries, possibly dating back to 520. It was attacked a number of times by Vikings and an entry in the *Annals of Ireland* in 802 states: "Inis Muireadhaigh was burned by foreigners, and they attacked Ros Commain." The reference is to a Viking attack at Inishmurray and Roscommon and it is one of the earliest written records of such an episode.

© Office of Public Works

Inishmurray Island was the location of the first Viking raid in Ireland

earliest phase of activity, the twelfth-century round tower and St Molaise's house with their Romanesque decoration, and Teampall Mor the lower church dating to the thirteenth century. It appears that there were two separate monastic communities on the island and the remains of St Mary's Augustinian Priory date to the fifteenth and early sixteenth centuries.

There were further raids during the ninth and tenth centuries including one at Devenish Island on Lough Erne. The beautifully preserved round tower there is an example of a feature of Irish monasteries built to defend against Irish and Viking invaders. The towers served as monuments to the faith and although believed to be used primarily as bell towers, they were also sometimes used to keep monastic treasures safe.

The general perception of the Vikings as bloodthirsty, pillaging and plundering pirates comes mainly from annalists who recorded the attacks. However, the Vikings also brought expertise in shipbuilding, an expansion of foreign trade, coinage, towns and were a strong influence on Irish life and politics.

## Gaelic lordships

In the Early Medieval period (the fifth to the twelfth century) some people lived in ringforts, cashels and crannógs, and there is increasing evidence to suggest that they continued to live in these settlement forms after the arrival of the Anglo-Normans in 1169.

There were a number of powerful Gaelic-Irish families in Bréifne during this time. Medieval Gaelic society is referred to as a clan or lineage based society. Land was held by the extended family group rather than the individual and was periodically redistributed amongst members of the family group. The economy remained largely pastoral. Barter, especially in cattle,

© National Library of Ireland

A depiction of a feast in Gaelic Ireland in the late sixteenth century was the most frequent method of business transaction. Towns and villages were not established and settlements were for the most part dispersed. The Gaelic-Irish did not tend to construct large masonry castles until the fifteenth century, when they began to construct tower houses – three to five storey rectangular or occasionally circular stone towers, often surrounded by a walled stone enclosure called a bawn.

## Anglo-Norman legacy

The Anglo-Normans arrived in Ireland in 1169 to help the deposed king of Leinster, Dermot MacMurrough, regain his kingdom. The knights who came were granted large areas of Ireland and many of them encouraged English, Welsh, French and Flemish settlers to come to the country. Large areas of Bréifne, however, were never settled by the Anglo-Normans and remained under Gaelic-Irish control. Other areas of Bréifne were colonised by the Anglo-Normans soon after their arrival in Ireland but were soon regained by the Gaelic-Irish. Sligo town for

Image ©National Museum of Ireland

example, was established by the Anglo-Normans in 1236, but by 1333 it was under Gaelic-Irish control.

Anglo-Norman lords constructed earthwork castles in the twelfth and thirteenth centuries, both at the centre of the areas of land they had been granted and at the borders of their areas of control. The motte and baileys at Kilmore, near Cavan town, and Turbet Island in Belturbet were part of an unsuccessful attempt by the Anglo-Normans to expand their area of control. A motte is a steep-sided mound of earth with a flat top. Described as pudding-bowl in shape, some mottes like those at Kilmore and Turbet Island, had an attached enclosed area called a bailey which would have contained houses and other buildings. Originally, there would have been a wooden tower and palisade on top of the motte, which would have served as the place of last resort during attack.

The Anglo-Normans were also responsible for the construction of a number of masonry castles in Bréifne. Clough Oughter Castle (see p16) is the ruin of a large thirteenth-century circular keep on a small island in Lough Oughter while another Anglo-Norman castle was built in Ballymote around 1300 (see p78) and was captured by the Irish some 20 years later.

## English and Scottish settlers

In the sixteenth and seventeenth centuries the English Crown adopted a policy of plantation in an attempt to secure and tighten political control over Ireland. English and Scottish settlers considered loyal to the Crown were granted ownership of the land formerly held by the Gaelic-Irish and Anglo-Irish. Attempts to plant Ulster had failed in the sixteenth century but the Flight of the Earls in 1607, which saw the exodus of the Earls of Tyrconnell, Tyrone and other Ulster noblemen, created a situation in which a more successful plantation could be planned. Across Bréifne today some of the plantation castles and fortified houses that were the homes of the English and Scottish remain upstanding today. For example, the fortified houses in Dromahair and Manorhamilton were built by settlers and villages often grew up around these settlements, as was the case with Tully Castle (see p79).

From the houses and towns of the planters, to the evidence left by the first settlers and the Gaelic chieftains, to the motte and bailey castles of the Normans there are many places of interest where today's visitors can see and learn more about these times. At almost every turn Bréifne will tell a story relating to the origin, footprint and settlements left by many peoples over thousands of years.

The O'Crean tomb in Sligo Abbey has beautiful carved figures

**The fortified house in Dromahair was built during the period of the Plantation of Ireland by English and Scottish settlers**

## Great Castles of Bréifne

### Ballymote Castle

This is the most impressive Anglo-Norman castle in Bréifne. Approximately 28km from the gateway city of Sligo, it was built around 1300 by the Anglo-Norman lord Richard de Burgo and captured by the Irish only 20 years after its completion. It remained in their control until 1584 when it was taken by the notorious Richard Bingham, then Governor of Connaught. For a time it was in the possession of the O'Donnells and it was from here that Red Hugh O'Donnell set out to take part in the Battle of Kinsale in 1601. The castle consists

**Ballymote Castle**

of an almost square courtyard surrounded by high stone walls with corner towers on each angle and D-shaped towers midway along the west and east walls. Excavations suggest it may once have been surrounded by a shallow moat. *The Book of Ballymote*, a fourteenth-century manuscript written mostly in Gaelic, and containing genealogical, topographical and biblical material and a key to the Ogham alphabet, was written here.

### Monea Castle

Monea Castle is the best preserved plantation castle in Bréifne and was constructed around 1619. Located just outside the village of Derrygonnelly, it was badly damaged in an attack by the Maguires during the 1641 uprising and was abandoned in the early 1700s. It shows architectural features reflecting the Scottish or English origin of the settlers. The main building forms the south-east boundary of the bawn enclosure, which also featured two flanking towers. The west side of the castle features two circular towers, with the entrance to the castle located between them. The uppermost part of the towers support a square chamber, and are similar to towers from Claypotts Castle in Fife, Scotland.

**Monea Castle**

## Parke's Castle

This seventeenth-century fortified house is near Dromahair on the shores of Lough Gill. It is built on the site of the sixteenth-century O'Rourke tower house.

The fortified house was constructed by Captain Robert Parke after 1628, when he was granted the land as part of the plantation of Leitrim. Parke dismantled the tower house, the foundations of which are visible in the castle courtyard. The fortified house incorporates the east section of the bawn wall, and the gatehouse of the original castle complex forms the southernmost part of the house. Two Scottish-type turrets were positioned at the corners of the bawn wall overlooking Lough Gill. The seventeenth-century castle was originally called Newtown and there would have been village houses beneath the castle walls, as well as a church for the settlement. The excavations at the castle, which uncovered the stone footings of the tower house, also revealed the remains of a blacksmith's forge, a well, and a sallyport or water-gate to the lake. The castle has undergone extensive renovations by the Irish Government's Office of Public Works.

Boat tours on Lough Gill depart from the jetty adjacent to the castle and include the Lake Isle of Inishfree with its commentary on Yeats and his poetry.

Parke's Castle

## Tully Castle

Situated on the shores of Lower Lough Erne, Tully Castle was constructed around 1613 by Sir John Hume who had been granted lands in the area as part of the Plantation of Ulster. It consists of a plantation castle and a surrounding bawn wall. Although the castle is built in a Scottish style, the method of construction (the use of random-rubble masonry) would indicate that Irish masons were used to build it. The castle is two storeys high with attic rooms above and stands at almost its full original height. The main reception rooms of the house would have been on the first floor, with the bedrooms in the attics above. The ground floor would have housed the kitchen and a store. Tully Castle was burned by the Maguires in 1641 and the house was probably never rebuilt as the family moved to Castle Hume nearer Enniskillen. The castle is surrounded by seventeenth-century-style gardens which were replanted within the bawn.

Tully Castle

Enniskillen Castle on the island which gives the town its name

# ENNISKILLEN - BELLEEK - BLACKLION-BELCOO

## Enniskillen

The development of Enniskillen and the history of the area are intimately linked with the Erne Waterway. The town itself developed around a castle built by the Maguires in the fifteenth century, but this fording point on the River Erne was probably in use from a much earlier period. Stone axes, Bronze Age swords and Iron Age ornaments have been found on the riverbed downstream close to Portora Castle. Throughout the millennia people have settled along the Erne waterways and the long span of human presence in Enniskillen can be seen at various sites, both in the town and its hinterland.

Enniskillen, or in Gaelic *Inis Ceithleann*

A traditional shopfront in Enniskillen

(Ceithle's Island), is situated more or less in the centre of Co Fermanagh on a natural island that is formed between Upper Lough Erne and Lower Lough Erne.

The colourful costumes of visiting mummers performing in The Diamond

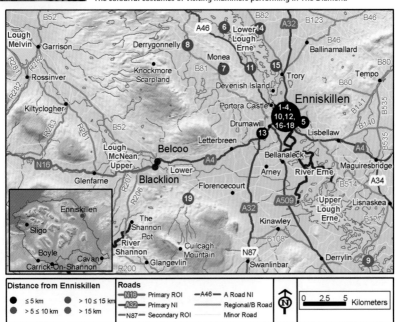

| Distance from Enniskillen | | Roads | |
|---|---|---|---|
| ● ≤ 5 km | ● > 10 ≤ 15 km | N16 Primary ROI / A32 Primary NI / N87 Secondary ROI | A46 A Road NI / Regional/B Road / Minor Road |
| ● > 5 ≤ 10 km | ● > 15 km | | |

0  2.5  5  Kilometers

© National Library Ireland

Town Hall Street in Enniskillen in the late nineteenth century

A bustling commercial area, Enniskillen is one of the principal towns in the north-west of Ireland. The town boasts a great range of shops and pubs, but still manages to retain a sense of traditional Irish charm and character. Attractions include historic buildings such as Enniskillen Castle, heritage and craft centres, museums, woodland parks and walking trails. As it is a unique island town, there is a strong focus on cruising, angling and all sorts of water-based activity. The area is a hub for cruising on the Erne system and onwards into the Shannon-Erne Waterway and the greater Shannon system, offering over 800km of navigable waters (see p149).

Enniskillen is 177km from Dublin on the N3, followed by the A509 into the town. From Belfast take the M1 west and then follow the A4.

## Accommodation and eating out

As expected in a town of its size, there is tourist accommodation to suit every budget, including B&Bs, hotels and a youth hostel. Popular places to stay include the Fort Lodge Hotel, the four-star Killyhevlin Hotel on the edge of Lough Erne and the Railway Hotel convenient to activities and attractions.

Excellent restaurants, bistros, coffee shops, tea rooms, cafés and sandwich bars mean Enniskillen provides a wide choice of eating-out options. Seafood is a local speciality.

## Information point

**1. Tourist Information Centre**
Wellington Road, Enniskillen
T: 0044 (0)28 6632 3110
W: www.fermanaghlakelands.com

**2. Enniskillen Castle and Museums**
T: 0044 (0)28 6632 5000
W: enniskillencastle.co.uk
This imposing castle is actually made up of a number of different buildings from different times, reflecting its long and varied history. The castle was founded by the Gaelic Maguire chieftains, and the family ruled the area from this stronghold. Today the castle represents an important part of Fermanagh's history and heritage. It was refurbished and remodelled in 1607 under Captain William Cole. The castle now houses both

The Diamond in Town Hall Street

Enniskillen has lots of nice pubs, including Blake's

Summer sports always include Gaelic football

the Regimental Museum and Fermanagh County Museum. The Regimental Museum, in the former castle keep, illustrates the military history of the site that was home to the Inniskilling Regiment (see p84). Fermanagh County Museum is housed in a modern heritage centre built within the castle complex and some 8,000 artefacts are included in the collection as well as a large photographic collection and oral history recordings and transcripts. An exhibition gives an insight into Fermanagh's natural history, archaeology and rural lifestyle.

### 3. Cole's Monument

The statue at Forthill Park is of the son of the Earl of Enniskillen, Sir Galbraith Lowry Cole (1772-1842). He was one of Wellington's generals in the Peninsular War. The climb of 108 steps to the top of the monument is rewarded by panoramic views of the area and the monument is visible from many vantage points in the town.

### 4. Saint Macartan's Cathedral and Saint Michael's Church

Saint Macartan's Church of Ireland Cathedral, sits on the site of a church built in 1627 by William Cole, founder of the town. Very little remains of the original building but an inscription stone from 1637 can be seen over the door. The present building was designed by Thomas Elliott and opened in 1842. It is

The stained glass images in Saint Michael's Church

characteristic of early Victorian architecture. The flags of the Inniskilling Fusiliers and Dragoons are displayed in the Cathedral and volunteers provide guided tours.

Saint Michael's Catholic Church across the street is of the French Gothic revival style and was dedicated on Saint Patrick's Day 1875. Outstanding murals by Scottish artist Charles Russell are on the left side of the church and the church is also noted for its magnificent stained glass windows and high altar.

Scoff's Restaurant and Wine Bar is one of the many fine place to eat in Enniskillen

## 5. Castle Coole

🏠🛏️🚐♿ℹ️❄️CC🅿️£🔒

📷 This impressive house set in a 700-acre estate is a National Trust treasure. Tours of the house are

A summer bounty from one of Ireland's most beautiful regions

available and walks in the grounds reveal the Grand Yard, ice house, dairy, stables and a display room which houses the Belmore Coach (see p15).

## 6. Inishmacsaint

🏠🏛️ The remains of a monastery founded by St Ninnid, an important Fermanagh bishop, can be accessed by boat to the island on Lower Lough Erne, or on foot via a pontoon.

There is also a striking high cross, distinctive because it lacks the usual Celtic circle. St Ninnid is said to have lived on Inishmacsaint sometime around 530. He has strong associations with Lough Erne in general, with a holy well dedicated to him in Belleek and also at Knockninny pier on Upper Lough Erne.

The high cross at Inishmacsaint is unusual in an Irish context as it lacks the Celtic circle normally associated with these crosses

# The Inniskillings' Museum

**T:** 0044 (0)28 6632 5000
**W:** enniskillencastle.co.uk

🏠🏛️♿ℹ️❄️🛏️CC🅿️£

Enniskillen is the only town to have given its name to two regiments in the British Army. The Inniskillings' Museum located within Enniskillen Castle tells the story of the two regiments. These regiments, one of foot soldiers, called the Royal Inniskilling Fusiliers, and one of cavalry (dragoons) called the Royal Inniskilling Dragoon Guards, have their origins in the late seventeenth century.

In the time of the English civil war, when Ireland was in turmoil during the conflict between the armies of King James and King William, volunteer forces were raised to defend the town. Two of these regiments were incorporated in the British Army, and for almost 300 years carried the name Inniskilling in their titles. The town's name has had many different English spellings over the years and the spelling of the regiments' names originates in the Gaelic name for Enniskillen. Throughout their illustrious history the regiments

have taken part in most of the major campaigns and battles fought on behalf of the British Empire. At Waterloo, the 27th (Inniskilling) Regiment of Foot was brought from the rear and told to form square in the centre of the allied line and in doing so suffered some 66 per cent casualties. All their officers bar one were killed or wounded. The Duke of Wellington is reported to have stated that "they saved the centre of my line", while Napoleon is supposed to have said that "We had the day won, save for those stubborn mules with the castles in their caps." The 6th (Inniskilling) Dragoons, in the Union Brigade, took part in a crucial cavalry charge and also suffered heavy casualties.

The museum has fine displays of weapons, uniforms and vehicles which are used to tell the story of the regiments. The many medals on show bring alive the story of individuals, and the magnificent silver evokes scenes of ceremony and splendour. The museum has an audio-visual virtual tour on the ground floor for visitors with a disability.

The history of the Inniskillings' can be enjoyed at Enniskillen Castle

## 7. Monea Castle

🗙 ▣ ♿ Perhaps the best preserved and complete plantation castle in Ulster, Monea Castle features two Scottish style semi-circular towers, topped by box-like turrets, which may have been designed to resemble a gatehouse (see p78).

## 8. Field Study Centre

**T:** 0044 (0)28 6864 1673
**W:** field-studies-council.org
ℹ️ ♿ cc P £ ♿ ☺ The Field Study Centre at Derrygonnelly, the only centre in Northern Ireland operated by the UK Field Studies Council organisation, provides residential and day courses in environmental studies. An excellent variety of habitats are within easy reach of the centre including rocky shores, freshwater, sand dunes, rivers, bog and heathland as well as carboniferous limestone, shale, intrusive igneous rocks and glacial deposits.

## 9. Inish Rath Island Visitor Centre, Derrylin

♿ ℹ️ The peace of this island in Upper Lough Erne is what drew the Hare Krishna community that now lives there. They have restored a section of a nineteenth-century Victorian mansion as a visitors' centre. The island also offers wooded walks, the marvels of the temple, and treasures and crafts.

## 10. The Buttermarket Centre

ℹ️ ♿ ▣ cc P The Buttermarket is in the old area of town where all farming transactions took place in the nineteenth and early twentieth century and was once a thriving corn and buttermarket.

The fireworks display in Enniskillen at Hallowe'en

It is now used by a wide selection of artists and craftspeople who have premises there (see p168).

## Festivals and events

The town's best known festivals are the Enniskillen Drama Festival in March, the BorderTrek cycling event, the World Water-Skiing Championships and the Fermanagh Classic Fishing Festival. The Erne Vintage Car Rally every August is popular with car enthusiasts. There is also the Lady of the Lake Festival (Irvinestown) in July and a festival in Kesh in August featuring music,

activities, street games and a carnival queen dance.

## Golf

**11/12/13/14.** The Castle Hume Championship Golf Course is situated on the banks of Lower Lough Erne, only a few minutes drive out of Enniskillen town centre. Enniskillen Golf Club was established in 1896, and is a superb 18-hole parkland course set beside Castle Coole Estate. Courses are also located at the Ashwoods Golf Centre and the Manor House Hotel and Leisure Complex.

Enniskillen has a wide variety of festivals throughout the year

## 19. Marble Arch Caves European Geopark

**T:** 0044 (0)28 6634 8855
**W:** marblearchcaves.com
**Open:** March-September

Located in the north of Bréifne, close to the villages of Florencecourt, Blacklion and Belcoo, Marble Arch Caves are one of Europe's finest showcave systems. They are a world-class, natural attraction containing marvellous stream passages formed by three rivers that sink underground on the slopes of Cuilcagh Mountain. These rivers disappear into the limestone on the lower slopes of the mountain and unite in the caves to re-emerge as the Cladagh River at Marble Arch, a natural rock bridge spanning the river.

Edouard Martel, the French speleologist (cave scientist) carried out the first daring exploration of the caves in 1895. Together with Lyster Jameson, a young student of bats from the Royal Irish Academy in Dublin, Martel paddled along in the dark, foreboding cave river and clambered among immense boulders by candlelight to draw the first maps of the cave.

Due to their internationally important landscapes, in 2001 both Marble Arch Caves and Cuilcagh Mountain Park were jointly recognised by UNESCO (the United Nations Educational, Scientific and Cultural Organisation), as one of the first European Geoparks. In 2004 they were recognised as a UNESCO Global Geopark.

The geology of the Marble Arch Caves European Geopark has helped to create a patchwork of rare, natural habitats. Some of the last remaining natural areas of damp ash woodland in Ireland are found along rivers that rise out of the mountain. Limestone grassland is present on the lower slopes of Cuilcagh Mountain, hosting a unique community of wild flowers, animals and insects. Blanket bog up to two and three metres thick can be found elsewhere, covering the landscape with a deep cloak of peat; a gigantic natural sponge covering the bedrock.

Peat was cut from the blanket bogs of Cuilcagh Mountain for many centuries. For hundreds of years local people used sleans (adapted spades) to cut the peat they needed to burn in their cottage hearths,

causing limited damage to the bog. However, in the mechanised age of the late twentieth century, large-scale, industrial peat cutting severely damaged the fragile bog ecosystem. An active conservation programme is restoring the blanket bog, now protected under European environment laws as an endangered habitat.

Some 60,000 people visit the Marble Arch Caves European Geopark for guided tours, hill-walking or motor-touring in the countryside. Field study programmes attract thousands of school children, university students or enthusiastic adults wanting to learn more about the caves, limestone and bog environments of this amazing corner of Ireland.

Guided tours of Marble Arch Caves allow visitors to safely explore this underworld, first by boat past rocky walls along a subterranean river and then by walking past bewitching arrays of glistening stalactites, stalagmites and flowstones. In high season it is advisable to ring ahead to book a place on the tours, which take place every 15 minutes.

Part of the tour in Marble Arch Caves includes an unusual boat trip while underground

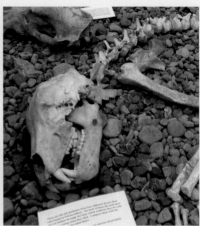
Bones of the brown bear on display at Marble Arch Caves

Some of the stalactites formed over 50,000 years ago and grow at the incredibly slow rate of less than one millimetre per year. The large stalactite is called after Edouard Martel who first explored the caves

## Portora Royal School and Castle

Oscar Wilde

Samuel Beckett

Portora Royal School in Enniskillen boasts Oscar Wilde and Samuel Beckett as past pupils. Wilde spent much of his youth in Enniskillen and attended the school from 1864. Not surprisingly, the boy who went on to write plays such as *The Importance of Being Earnest* and novels like *The Picture of Dorian Gray* excelled in the classics, taking top prizes. It has been said that Wilde drew inspiration for his fairy tale *The Happy Prince* from Cole's Monument which stands in the Fort Hill Pleasure Grounds in Enniskillen.

The playwright Samuel Beckett excelled at cricket and began his studies of French at Portora. Perhaps his most well known work is *En attendant Godot (Waiting for Godot)*. He won the Nobel Prize for Literature and influenced a generation of dramatists.

Nearby Portora Castle was built in 1614 on the banks of Lower Lough Erne by Sir William Cole, and consists of a three-storey house surrounded by a defensive wall, which had a circular tower at each of its four corners.

### 15. Helicopter rides
T: 0044 (0)48 6632 9000

Trip-of-a-lifetime pleasure flights and tours over Bréifne and beyond are available at Enniskillen Airport. Flying lessons and instruction are also available.

### 16. Erneside Shopping Centre
T: 0044 (0)28 6632 7114
One of the few large shopping centres in Ireland where boats and cruisers can be moored nearby, Erneside is a modern retail development with a variety of shops.

### 17. Fermanagh Lakeland Forum
T: 0044 (0)28 6632 4121
The forum has something to offer everyone. There are indoor and outdoor play areas, a restaurant, regular events and numerous activities. The soft play area is popular with small children while the swimming pool, fitness suite and steam room appeal to all ages.

### 18. Ardhowen Theatre
T: 0044 (0)28 6632 5440
The Ardhowen provides a year round programme to suit all tastes, and includes drama, classical music, opera, ballet, comedy, country music, mime, traditional Irish music and dance, as well as arts and lectures. The theatre is situated in a panoramic lake view setting on the outskirts of Enniskillen and its restaurant is an award-winning member of the Healthy Eating Circle. An events brochure with comprehensive details of all performances can be obtained by contacting the Ardhowen or from many other outlets throughout Bréifne.

## Walking

The local tourism office has details of walks throughout Fermanagh. There is a selection of woodland, hill and lakeshore trails that offer an opportunity to enjoy some of the wildlife and scenery of the area.

Ardhowen Theatre has regular big name acts including the Three Tenors

## Aughakillymaude Mummers

Mumming involves troupes of local volunteer actors creating enjoyable and chaotic community folk dramas in houses, streets, pubs and halls, and the Aughakillymaude Mummers are a fine illustration of this important folk tradition in Bréifne.

The ancient tradition of mumming has pagan origins

Laden with symbolism, it is thought the tradition was brought to Ireland during the eleventh and twelfth centuries and was originally pagan. The plays are traditionally performed during mid-winter and they are also associated with weddings and Christmas. Mummers are said to bring luck to wherever they perform.

The 'hero combat play,' where a warrior or saint kills an adversary, who is then revived by a comic doctor, is the most common mummer performance. The actors wear outlandish straw costumes and tall, conical straw masks, which are thought to be linked to guarding against being seen and abducted by fairies, witches or bad spirits.

The main characters of the plays in Bréifne include St Patrick, Cromwell, White Horse (a Celtic fertility symbol who bites women to ensure reproduction within six months), Bold Slasher (an Irish knight who boasts of his bravery on the battlefield when defending Ireland against the British), and Old Biddy Funny, an old hag who threatens people for money.

The Aughakillymaude Mummers (Aughakillymaude means 'the Wooden Field of the Wild Dog') are famous for bringing diversion and mayhem wherever they appear. Their old national school first built in 1888, now contains a cultural and activity centre explaining the history of the tradition.

The Aughakillymaude Mummers

# Belleek

Belleek was founded as part of the Plantation of Ulster in the early seventeenth century by Thomas Blennerhasset and his brother, Sir Edward, of Norfolk. The Blennerhassets remained in Belleek until 1662 when they sold the estate and the castle they had built to Sir James Caldwell. The Caldwell's house and estate, which included the town of Belleek, was named Castle Caldwell. The estate is now a forest park and is open to the public.

Belleek, or in Gaelic *Béal Leice* (River-Mouth of the Flagstone), marks the end of the Shannon-Erne navigation system. The picturesque village sits on the River Erne in the north-west corner of Bréifne. Lough Melvin and Lower Lough Erne dominate the landscape of the surrounding area. To the south-east are drumlin hills, while the land to the east rises to the plateau of the Lough Navar and Ballintempo Uplands, forming spectacular cliff faces such as the Cliffs of Magho. West of Belleek lies an undulating landscape of bogs and farmland, ending in a short rocky stretch of coastline.

Belleek holds a special place in the hearts of china collectors all over the world. As the home of Ireland's oldest pottery since the 1850s, the village is famous for its distinctive Parian china. As a result the area hosts a cosmopolitan tourist population and many return

The Thatch on the main street in Belleek is a great place to enjoy a snack

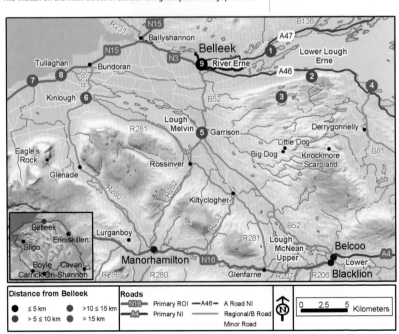

Belleek circa 1900                     © National Library of Ireland

to the village year after year. Activities to be enjoyed in Belleek range from cruising and cycling to heritage tours and fishing. Belleek is also well known as a venue for traditional Irish music and welcomes travelling musicians. The three-day Belleek Summer Traditional Music Festival is held in June.

Belleek is accessed via the A46 from Enniskillen, and on the N15 or N16-R82-B52 out of Sligo.

## Accommodation and eating out

The 35-bed Hotel Carlton in the town is family run and set in a wonderfully scenic location and has spa and wellness centre facilities. There are also a number of lodges, guesthouses, B&Bs and self-catering cottages to pick from.

Places to eat in the town include the Saimer Restaurant and the Potters Bar in Hotel Carlton, Moohan's Fiddlestone, an old-time country pub, and McDonnell's Café on Main Street.

There are extensive opportunities to enjoy a day's fishing on the Erne lakes

## Information point

### Tourist Information Centre
🛈 Wellington Road
Enniskillen
**T:** 0044 (0)28 6632 3110
**W:** fermanaghlakelands.com
**Open:** All year

### The Lough Erne Waterways
🎏🚣 A superb natural resource, Lough Erne attracts a lot of visitors due to the diversity of water sports, fishing and the beautiful

surrounding scenery. There are numerous islands all around the lake, which can be visited by boat for excursions and picnics. The Gaelic name, *Loch Éirne*, means 'the Lake of the Erni'. The Erni was an ancient mythical tribe of the Fir Bolg, said to have lived in the plain before it was flooded and the lake formed.

Both Upper and Lower Lough Erne provide magnificent waterways for unrestricted cruising and boating and are amongst the least congested in Europe. Cruisers can be hired in both Belleek and Enniskillen.

The lakeside is high and rocky in some parts and, in addition to the numerous islands, there are coves, historic sites, castle ruins and stately homes to explore. Common breeding birds include snipe, curlew, redshank and sandwich terns. In winter the lakes are an important site for whooper swans. The vast shallows and rocky areas provide ideal conditions for brown trout and bream, eel, perch and roach and Lough Erne has claimed many world coarse angling match records. (see p146).

Upper and Lower Lough Erne are a dominating influence on the life of Fermanagh

## 9. Belleek Pottery

**T:** 0044 (0)28 6865 9300     **W:** belleek.ie

Situated at the north-eastern tip of Lough Erne, the world famous Belleek Pottery Centre is a favourite stop for many visitors. The idea for the pottery first came in 1849 when John Caldwell Bloomfield returned home to Ireland from China, having inherited Castle Caldwell Estate. His main interest was mineralogy and he was considered to be an accomplished amateur, whose knowledge extended to a keen appreciation of ceramics. He took more than a passing notice of the unique glistening white finish on the walls of the thatched-roofed homes on his estate. Bloomfield knew the covering was limestone, but it was the unusual sparkle that he found most intriguing.

In 1852 Bloomfield commissioned a geological survey of his estate, which found significant quantities of feldspar on his land, followed by china clay, and kaolin, all required ingredients for the making of pottery. He subsequently teamed up with Robert Williams Armstrong, an Irish engineer who was working for the Royal Porcelain Works at Worcester, and they began producing feldspar for their plant. The success of this led the pair to establish their own ceramic plant in Belleek. The site chosen for the plant was Rose Island on Lough Erne, which ensured an unlimited water supply for manufacturing, powered a massive water-wheel, and also facilitated transporting raw materials in and finished goods out.

After successfully recruiting expert staff from UK potteries to supplement and train the local workforce Belleek Pottery began to develop the distinctive fine Parian china it is famed for to this day. In 1865 the Pottery won its first gold medal at the Dublin International Exhibition and by 1869, the Art Journal thought that "the pottery's Parian creations had advanced to perfection." International acclaim was soon to follow, particularly when Queen Victoria presented a Belleek Tea Service to the German royal family. Belleek had its first official showing in America at the Philadelphia International Exhibition of 1876, and a second gold medal was awarded at the Melbourne International Exhibition of 1880.

For well over one hundred years the craftspeople in Belleek have continued to produce its famous lines of seashell designs, basket weaves and marine themes. It has become a favoured tradition in Ireland to give a piece of Belleek china as a wedding gift and this is also hugely popular in the US. The company has survived through the death of its founders, the difficulties of raw material supplies in both world wars and several changes of ownership.

Today Belleek Pottery employs about 120 people and its visitor centre has become one of the top tourist attractions in the region. Visitors can enjoy a factory tour and see the craftspeople working, visit the museum and restaurant and enjoy one of Ireland's longest craft traditions.

**Hand painting Belleek Pottery**

## 1. Castle Caldwell

An RSPB reserve with wildfowl hides, walks, castle ruins, woodland and picnic sites, the castle was for 300 years the home of the Caldwells, landlords of Belleek. The marked nature trails and walks are maintained by the Forestry Service, although parts of the forest are private. There is a visitor centre and marina.

## 2. The Cliffs of Magho

Overlooking Lower Lough Erne on the road between Enniskillen and Belleek, the cliffs are 9km long, cresting at over 300m. At the base of the cliff is semi-natural woodland, while further up are pockets of grassland, heath and scrub. The rare yellow mountain saxifrage, probably present from the last Ice Age, grows here. There is a steep trail to the cliff top off the Enniskillen road, 24km from Belleek. The cliffs may also be reached by taking the driving route through Lough Navar Forest.

## 3. Lough Navar Forest

The Lough Navar scenic drive on the Garrison to Derrygonelly road goes through Lough Navar Forest to the viewpoint over the Cliffs of Magho. There are car parking facilities, picnic areas, viewpoints and short walks. Opposite the entrance to Lough Navar Forest, there is a nature trail along the banks of the Sillees River which runs through the Correl Glen Nature Reserve.

## 4. Tully Castle

This is a well preserved example of an early seventeenth-century plantation castle and well worth a visit. The site is open to the public and a cottage at the site has been rebuilt and is now used as an information centre (see p79). It is located on the road between Enniskillen and Belleek on the shores of Lough Erne.

## 5. Lough Melvin and Lough Melvin Holiday Centre, Garrison

T: 0044 (0)28 6865 8142
Lough Melvin, 13km by 3km with several large islands, is an angler's paradise as it is probably the last lake in Europe with populations of the ferox, sonaghan and gillaroo wild brown trout species. Arctic char, the rare Atlantic salmon, as well char and perch are also present (see p108).

Lough Melvin Holiday Centre has hostel and caravanning facilities and also offers windsurfing, sailing, canoeing, surfing, mountain biking, caving, hiking and other similar activities.

## 6. Annals of the Four Masters

The town of Kinlough stands at the western end of Lough Melvin. It was in the town's Ross Friary that the seventeenth-century *Annals of the Kingdom of Ireland*, one of the principal Irish historical sources, was compiled. Its writers were known as the Four Masters and a bronze memorial to them stands on the Four Masters' Bridge, over the River Drowes at Mullanaleck.

## 7. The Bunduff holy wells

Two holy wells can be found near the mouth of the Duff River. St Patrick's Well is made up of an oval cairn with a small rectangular dry-stone well to its west side. Further west is Shaver's Well, a dry-stone well covered by a limestone slab and open to the north where it connects with a stream. Placing stones at a holy well was part of a tradition to mark the pilgrim's visit.

## Erne Heritage Tours

T: 0044 (0)28 686 58327
W: erneheritagetours.com
Erne Heritage Tours provide personalised tours as well as assistance with genealogy research, local heritage and history.

## 8. Tullaghan Cross

The Tullaghan Cross, seen on the N15 travelling from Sligo in the direction of Bundoran, was moved to this location from the coast to protect it from erosion. It is believed to be part of a long vanished monastery. Tradition records that the Tullaghan Cross was washed up upon the foreshore after a storm and was erected at its current location by a local landowner, Thomas Dickson. The base on which the cross now stands and the inscribed date, 1778, were added at this time. A trip to Tullaghan is also rewarded with panoramic views of the Tievebaun, Truskmore and Arroo mountains.

The Tullaghan Cross dates from the eleventh or twelfth centuries

Image ©Office of Public Works

## Big Dog and Little Dog - Fionn's two wolfhounds

On the road between Derrygonnelly and Garisson two small but prominent hills are noticeable features of the landscape. They are known locally as Big Dog and Little Dog (*Sliabh Dà Chon* or the Mountain of the Two Hounds) and while geologists tell us they are made of hard sandstone, local folklore has a different explanation. It is said that Fionn MacCumhail, leader of Na Fianna, once passed this way with his two dogs, Bran and Sceolan, two Irish wolfhounds. As they travelled over the Fermanagh hills, the two dogs took off after a witch who, in an attempt to outrun them, turned herself into a doe. However the dogs continued to gain on her and in her desperation, she cast a spell turning them into rock. Ever since, the lonely landscape of west Fermanagh has been the resting place for Bran and Sceolan, the Big Dog and the Little Dog.

# Blacklion and Belcoo

Blacklion is called after an inn of the same name that stood on an old coach road in the village. Its official Gaelic name *An Blaic* originates from that time but has no meaning in itself in the language, much like many other Gaelic names which were anglicised. Another Gaelic name *Learga* is also used for Blacklion.

Lough MacNean and the limestone crag known as Hanging Rock

Belcoo or *Béal Cú* (Mouth of the Narrow Neck of Land) takes the name from its location at the narrow stretch of river connecting Upper and Lower Lough MacNean. Belcoo owes its existence to the building of a railway station in 1848. A man named Hamilton Jones was one of the people responsible for bringing the railway there and for the creation of Belcoo as a town. He also built the first stone house in the town. The villages sit on each side of the neck of land separating Upper and Lower Lough MacNean. To the south of the lough the land rises to the Marlbank and Cuilcagh Mountain, while to the north lie the Knockmore Scarplands and Ballintempo Uplands. The upland landscape features steep cliffs, extensive bogs, bare limestone pavement, dry valleys, potholes, gorges, disappearing rivers, caves and springs. The lowlands are marked by clusters of rounded drumlins.

Charming twin villages, they straddle the border between the Republic of Ireland and Northern Ireland. The area around the two villages is rich in archaeological and heritage sites. Both villages

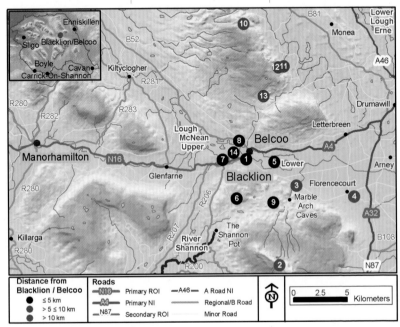

| Distance from Blacklion / Belcoo | | Roads | | | |
|---|---|---|---|---|---|
| ● | ≤ 5 km | N16 | Primary ROI | A46 | A Road NI |
| ● | > 5 ≤ 10 km | A4 | Primary NI | | Regional/B Road |
| ● | > 10 km | N87 | Secondary ROI | | Minor Road |

0   2.5   5 Kilometers

also lie close to Florence Court, one of the most famous 'big houses' in Ulster. The renowned Marble Arch Caves European Geopark, one of Europe's finest show cave systems, is also nearby. Popular activities in the area include walking, climbing, caving and scenic drives.

The villages are on the A4 out of Enniskillen and the N16, if approaching from Sligo and Manorhamilton, and are approximately 190km from Dublin and 150km from Belfast.

## Accommodation and eating out

The family-run Custom House in Belcoo is located on the main street at the foot of Cuilcagh Mountain. It overlooks the waters of Lough MacNean and offers dining and accommodation. Cassie Quinn's, an Irish-style restaurant, offers a wide menu choice while the Tully Hill Restaurant in Florencecourt, with its beautiful setting in the restored water mill, also offers fine food. Blacklion is something of a food-lover's destination as it is home to

Belcoo is a great location to enjoy some of the superb attractions of west Cavan and Fermanagh

MacNean House and Bistro, which is owned and run by Neven Maguire, one of Ireland's most famous chefs.

## Information point
**1. Blacklion Tourist Office**
🛈 Market House, Blacklion
**T:** 00353 (0)71 9853941
**W:** cavantourism.com
**Open:** Seasonal

**2. Cuilcagh Mountain**
Cuilcagh Mountain, which rises to 665m, is the highest point in Bréifne. Its distinctive table-top profile is easily identified from anywhere across the region and forms the focus of an area rich in geology, archaeology, folklore, flora and fauna. On the mountain there are extensive stretches of blanket bog which provides a good habitat for birds, in particular golden plover and merlin. It also supports a number of locally rare plant species. On the summit there is a circular prehistoric cairn that may cover a passage tomb. The many hidden caves are popular with cavers while the excellent walking trails enable hill-walkers to enjoy the rugged mountain terrain (see p152).

## Neven Maguire
**T:** 00353 (0)71 9853022
Blacklion presents an opportunity to enjoy the cooking of Neven Maguire, one of Ireland's leading chefs. The MacNean House and Bistro offers modern Irish cuisine, fine dining, vegetarian and seafood delights and makes extensive use of the local network of organic food producers. The Bistro offers overnight accommodation so the gastronomic pleasures can also be enjoyed at breakfast the following morning. There is a private dining room for the special occasion or group needs. It is an ideal touring base and minutes away from the Marble Arch Caves, the Burren Forest, Lough MacNean and the uplands of Ballintempo.

Neven Maguire in his kitchen at MacNean Bistro in Blacklion

Mid-summer morning in Blacklion

Cuilcagh Mountain holds a unique UNESCO designation due to its geological significance

Image ©Irish Bird Images

The uplands of Cuilcagh offer the ideal breeding habitat for the merlin, a small and lively falcon

### 3. Cladagh Glen
❄🔲⚡ There is a spectacular example of a spring, called the Cascades, emerging where the massive thick-bedded Dartry limestone meets the thinner beds of Glencar limestone in Cladagh Glen. The glen lies 100m below Marble Arch Caves visitor centre and takes its name from the Cladagh River which is formed in the depths of the caves.

### 4. Florence Court Forest Park and the Irish Yew
**T:** 0044 (0)28 6634 3032
**Open:** All year
♿❄🅿🔲⚡ Florence Court Forest Park, an area of over 3,000 acres of open mountain and blanket bog, supports a wide variety of flora and fauna and is bordered by large areas of

The original Irish yew

Autumn colours on Lough MacNean

forest and natural woodland. There are four forest trails through the park and three nature reserves in the area. The Irish yew differs from the common yew in having upright branches and a columnar habit. Two small trees with this characteristic were found by George Willis in Aghatirouke townland on the slopes of Cuilcagh Mountain sometime between 1740 and 1760. He gave one of these to the Earl of Enniskillen who planted it in Florence Court and this is the tree you can see today - the other tree died.

Cuttings were taken from the tree and propagated from about 1780. The parent tree is female and though male trees have occurred, the resulting seedlings do not usually show the columnar habit. Propagation has been entirely by cuttings from this tree and all the Irish Yews now commonly seen in estates and churchyards throughout Ireland, England and beyond are descendants of this tree.

The mother tree has grown more open and less columnar than the typical Irish yew owing to the numerous cuttings taken

from it and the shade of surrounding trees.

### 5. Lough MacNean Lower
❄🔲⚡ Opposite the police station in Belcoo is an attractive park on the shores of Lough MacNean Lower. Panels provide information on the history, ecology, archaeology, geology and visitor attractions in the region. It is a beautiful location to relax with a picnic and enjoy the lake views and the magnificent sight of Hanging Rock.

### 6. Burren Forest
🏰🔱❄🅿➕🔲⚡ The prehistoric complex at the Burren Forest has a dense concentration of archaeological remains, mainly Neolithic, Bronze Age and early Medieval, and holds fine examples of three of the four principal megalithic tomb types recognised in Ireland. The tombs, cairns, hut sites and pre-bog walls all suggest considerable settlement here in prehistory. The prevalence of such a wide variety of tomb types suggests that this was a sacred area from the late Neolithic period up until the early Bronze Age, from about 3000-1500 BC. The climate of that era was milder and the area's inhabitants could live on the

The Burren Forest is one of Irelands archaelogical treasures

elevated slopes of the mountains. A millennium or so later Ireland's climate changed and the uplands were abandoned and eventually covered by blanket bog. Among the archaeological remains are the Burren Portal Tomb and the Calf House Portal Tomb, the latter so called because it was converted into an animal shelter sometime at the end of the nineteenth century. Opposite this is a path leading to the exceptionally well-preserved Giant's Leap Wedge Tomb.

The forest is in the care of Coillte, a state-owned forestry company in the Republic of Ireland, and the whole area is one of immense archaeological significance.

### Cathal Bui Mac Giolla Gunna

Cathal Bui Mac Giolla Gunna (1680-1756) was a famous poet who spent considerable periods of his life travelling throughout Bréifne. He has an association with Blacklion and Belcoo, where each year in June-July there is a festival in his honour. He originally studied to be a priest but it was as a poet and raconteur that he made his name. Some 15 poems are attributed to him with the most famous being his 'An Bonnán Buí' ('The Yellow Bittern').

### 7. St Brigid's Stones

Killinagh Church, a short distance from Blacklion, is a typical medieval church with features that include a triple-light east window. Beyond its cemetery is a remarkable collection of sixteen bullaun stones (stones with man-made hollows). They may have been used to grind foodstuffs or dyes, and are claimed to have curative properties. These stones are known as St Brigid's Stones, and were once used as cursing stones.

### 8. Templerushin

Located just outside Belcoo on the road to Belleek this ruined medieval church and St Patrick's Well are enclosed in a walled graveyard which houses a bullaun stone. Local tradition reports that one of the church's windows was a leper window, through which lepers could observe the Mass without coming into contact with the rest of the congregation. St Patrick's Well was an important pilgrimage destination.

### 9. Killykeegan

Along the road between the Marble Arch Caves and Marlbank National Nature Reserve at Killykeegan there are interesting karst features (karst is a geological term for a distinctive type of landscape underlain by sink holes and drainages). They include the Monastir Gorge where the Aghinrawn River sinks into the Marble Arch system; the Sruh Coppa river, which also sinks into Marble Arch; and, Pollreagh, a huge doline or collapse feature, visible just east of Sruh Coppa Bridge. At Killykeegan there is a panoramic view of the surrounding landscape, including the knoll-like Clyhannagh Hill that stands out from the surrounding rocks.

### 10. Knockmore Scarpland

The Knockmore Scarpland is another spectacular karst area with extensive cave systems, limestone pavements and steep limestone cliffs that tower over the surrounding land. The Reyfad and Boho cave systems are both in this

St Brigid's stones in Killinagh are a feature of early Christian establishments and are believed to be cursing stones

Late summer over the wonderful landscape in the Ballintempo Uplands

area. The Reyfad system is one of the longest, known cave systems in Ireland, with almost 7km of explored passages.

## 11. Boho Church and High Cross

🏚️❖ Boho Church, south of Derrygonnelly, appears to have been the site of a monastery or nunnery since the Early Medieval period. The nearby Church of Ireland church was built in the eighteenth century and the medieval door in this church may originally have come from this church site. The Boho high cross is missing its ringed head, but the shaft of the cross is quite well preserved with depictions of biblical scenes still on it.

## 12. Reyfad Stones

🏚️❖ Rock carvings that could date from around 3000 BC can be seen near Boho Church. They are located high up on a narrow lane above the church on the eastern slope of Boho Mountain. The rocks, a collection of six limestone outcrops, five of which have cup and ring decorations on them, may be astronomical or fertility symbols.

## 13. Aghanaglack dual court tomb

🏚️❖ This interesting dual court tomb site consists of two chambered galleries set back to back and sharing a common end stone. The site was excavated in the 1930s and finds included a serpentine bead, flint and chert hollow scrapers, a beautiful flint javelin and pottery fragments. Cremated bones belonging to a child and young adult were also found.

## The Shannon Pot

Ireland's greatest river, the Shannon (*An Sionna*), rises near Glangevlin on the west side of Cuilcagh Mountain and flows south for some 358km before entering the sea at Limerick.

There are interesting folklore stories about the source of the Shannon, and one concerns a magical grove of hazelnut trees which encircled a small well at the location. The place was sacred to the gods of Ireland and it was forbidden to eat the nuts from the magical trees, which gave the power of foresight and all knowledge. However, a goddess of the Tuatha Dé Danann called Sionna and granddaughter of the great sea god Lir, greatly desired to sample the forbidden fruit of the hazelnut trees. One day she approached the sacred grove, but the well which it surrounded swelled up into a torrent of water and swept her down into the earth from which it sprang. The river that flowed from the well continues to flow to this day, and was named after her - *An Sionna*. The river's source is located halfway along the Glangevlin to Blacklion road and is signposted.

The Shannon Pot near Glangevlin, the source of the longest river in Ireland and England

## The Maguires

The Maguire (Maguidhir) clan was originally a branch of the Airgialla (an early medieval kingdom in Ulster), and from the thirteenth century its leaders began to emerge as important chieftains in the area of modern Co Fermanagh, to the east of Upper Lough Erne. The Maguires were allied with the O'Donnells, who helped them to dominate the whole Erne basin from Belleek in the north-west to the southern tip of Lough Erne.

From 1300 to 1600 the Maguires gave Fermanagh 15 rulers. Unusually among Gaelic-Irish clans, the succession passed directly from father to son until 1486. In Irish society the position of head of a clan could go to any member of the extended clan group, and this could lead to internal divisions and instability. The nature of the succession in the Maguire family created a remarkable level of stability which must have contributed to their success in the period. In 1486 Sean Maguire became the first member of the junior branch of the Maguire family to become 'the Maguire', or head of the family. The junior branch of the family held the chieftaincy almost uninterrupted until the Flight of the Earls in 1607. Indeed it was Cuconnacht Maguire who was the instigator of the earls' flight and who organised the ship to take them to Paris. The Flight of the Earls and the Plantation of Ulster marked the end of the Maguire dominance of Fermanagh.

The chieftains from the junior branch of the Maguire family often took the name Cuconnacht and this reflected their tendency to look west rather than north. Indeed the area west of the Erne, their territorial heartland, had traditionally been considered part of Connaught. The senior branch of the Maguires was concentrated on the eastern side of the lough and rarely took that name. It was the Maguires who built the first castle at the site of Enniskillen.

### 14. Blacklion Golf Club

This beautiful parkland course established in 1962 has been described as one of the best maintained nine-hole courses in Ireland. There are coppices of woodland and mature trees and a lake comes into play on three holes. There are fine views of Lough MacNean and the surrounding landscapes.

### The Cavan Way

The Cavan Way is a 26km walk, providing a pleasant hill and valley walking connection between the Leitrim Way at Dowra, a small village near the source of the River Shannon, and the Ulster Way at Blacklion village. The section from Blacklion to Shannon Pot is hill walking while the 'Pot' to Dowra is mainly road. Walkers also frequent the upland section between the Shannon Pot and Blacklion, which includes the Burren Forest area and its cemetery of ancient tombs, stone megaliths and monuments. There are fine views from the elevated upland areas.

The Reyfad Stone has some very unusual carvings

The Customs Post at Belcoo post 1921

Image © Western Education and Library Board

Union Wood and Cladagh Glen hold stands of native deciduous woodland

The Irish hare is a relatively common mammal in Bréifne and it is often seen in the uplands. It is a distinct subspecies and does not develop a white coat in winter.

Image ©Mike Brown

# THE ECOLOGY OF BRÉIFNE

Extensive uplands, a network of lakes and waterways, as well as a coastline with sandy beaches and rocky shores mean that a wide range of wildlife and distinctive habitats can be encountered in Bréifne all year round. This diversity is a result of varied geology and geography, a changing climate and millennia of farming and human habitation. Specialities of the region include a host of rare species (some found nowhere else in Ireland), and a number of plants and animals found at the northerly and southerly extremes of their range.

## Ice Age reminders

Some of the wildlife in this part of Ireland is a reminder of its colder past. Plants known as Arctic alpines can be found exclusively on steep north-facing cliffs on high mountains such as Ben Bulben and above the valleys of Gleniff and Glenade. Three such plants have their only Irish location in the Darty Mountains – the fringed sandwort, chickweed willowherb and alpine saxifrage. The rare yellow saxifrage can also be found in wet seeps and springs along the cliffs.

It is thought these plants may have been some of the first colonising species that followed the retreat of the glaciers at end of the last Ice Age over 13,000 years ago. Once abundant in Bréifne, these plants now commonly grow in alpine regions or at northerly latitudes. The improved climate of today means they are confined to only a handful of sites in Bréifne, so their presence is unusual.

Examples of glacial relict populations are not, however, confined only to the plant kingdom. Another remnant of the Ice Age is the Arctic char, a close relative of the salmon, and one of the early colonisers of Bréifne's rivers and lakes. It lived most of its adult life at sea, swimming up rivers to spawn. As the climate warmed around 10,000 years ago, it became land-locked, confined to deep, cool lakes such as Lough Melvin and unable to return to the sea as it still does at more northerly latitudes.

Many species of plant and animal did not reach Bréifne before rising sea levels cut off the land bridges that once existed between Ireland and Britain and the wider European

The Darty Mountain range is home to some spectacular flora

## Relics from the cold

© Andy Ferguson

The Arctic char

The area around the Dartry Mountains is noted for steep cliffs, particularly at Glencar, Glenade and Gleniff. This environment is home to a number of very rare Arctic alpine species, to be found nowhere else in Ireland. Fringed sandwort, chickweed willowherb and alpine saxifrage are all present here. This environment is floristically very important at a national level.

Another relic from the same period is the Arctic char, a fish found in deep, cool lakes such as Lough Melvin. They were the first of our native fish species to colonise Ireland and as they are now largely isolated in their respective loughs are becoming genetically unique.

The chickweed willowherb

The fringed sandworth

The alpine saxifrage

continent. As a result, various species common in Europe and Britain are not found in Ireland. This allows species in Bréifne to be observed in a wider range of habitats and locations than expected. The Irish or mountain hare is one such example. In Western Europe, it is found in mountainous areas but in Ireland it also occurs in the lowlands and along coasts, areas that in Europe would be inhabited by the brown hare, which is absent from Ireland.

## Uplands

Relatively remote and sparsely populated, the uplands of Bréifne are havens for wildlife, with extensive blanket bogs, cliffs and deep valleys. They are also a favourite destination for walkers. Many interesting hours can be spent exploring locations such as the Dartry Mountains (including the distinctive peaks of Ben Bulben and Benwiskin), Cuilcagh Mountain, the

Arigna Mountains, Sliabh an Iarainn, the Boleybrack Uplands, and the Bricklieve and Curlew Mountains. Upland blanket bog, a climatic peatland, is one of

the most common habitats of the summit plateaux. This landscape looks like it has a blanket of peat draped over it. It can only be formed and sustained in areas with

The uplands of Bréifne, like those of Cuilcagh Mountain, provide the breeding habitat for the golden plover where it will make its nest in the heather and on bog hummocks

## Butterflies & Moths

rainfall in excess of 1,200mm per annum and which have cool summers. Blanket bog vegetation is made up of low growing heathers, bog cottons and deer grass. Spongy wet conditions underfoot are due to the abundance of Sphagnum moss, which holds many times its weight in water. Small plants such as mosses, liverworts and lichens abound in this environment.

The nutrient-poor bog is a harsh environment for most plants but some specialised species have made it their home. Insect-eating plants, like sundew, overcome the lack of nutrients in the peat by supplementing their diets with protein digested from flies trapped on their sticky leaves. There are few mammals present, with the main exception being the Irish hare. Some bird species hold their preferred nesting sites in the uplands. At the top of the food chain are the predators like the merlin, while curlew and plover, normally associated with mudflats and marshes, nest here. Small bird species are few, although pipits and larks are common in summer. On shallow peat, and where the slope is too steep for blanket bog to develop, heath can be found. This vegetation is dominated by the dwarf shrubs, ling heather and bell heather that turn the hills purple in summer when in full bloom.

When compared with the waterlogged bog of the upland plateaux, the steep limestone slopes of the mountainsides provide not only a visual contrast but also a different suite of

1. The emperor moth is present on open moors, woods and heath. Its flight period is usually later March to early June.

2. The marsh fritillary prefers damp meadows and moors. Its flight period is early May to mid July.

3. The green hairstreak can be found up to 2,000m high in mountain areas. Its flight period is early April to late August.

4. The orange tip prefers damp flower-rich meadows and is on the wing between late March and late July.

5. The narrow bordered hawk moth is scarce and prefers unimproved grasslands and acid bogs. It mimicks the bumble bee and adults are active between mid May and mid June.

Images © Robert Thompson

Image ©Robert Thompson

## Lough Melvin specialists

Lough Melvin is situated in the north-west corner of Bréifne and holds a unique salmonid (salmon and trout family) fish community which originates from the end of the last Ice Age. Three distinct species of trout are found there – the sonaghan, the gillaroo and the ferox. They are identifiable by their colouring, spotting patterns and shapes. Each has a particular habitat preference in the lake. They also differ in their feeding preferences. The sonaghan prefers water fleas, pupae and larvae; the gillaroo feeds almost exclusively on bottom living animals like snails and shrimp, while the ferox, from age three onwards, prefers fish species like perch and Arctic char.

Ferox

Gillaroo

Sonaghan

© Andrew Ferguson

habitats, plants and animals. These drier slopes support calcareous grassland, alpine plants and often an abundance of orchids, while raven and peregrine find their home here. These grasslands are the nearest to natural grasslands in Bréifne. Although formed as a result of woodland clearance and maintained by light grazing, they have not been reseeded nor have had artificial fertiliser applied. As a result, they support a great variety of plants and insects. In some locations, exposed rock forms limestone pavement. This habitat is best seen at Killykeegan Nature Reserve. Between the rocks, patches of thin soils support a species-rich sward with blue moor grass, quaking grass and wild thyme all present. Other species have a more alpine character such as mountain avens and juniper. Growing in the fissures between these rocks are ferns including hart's tongue fern and the brittle bladder-fern, a species that is rare in Ireland.

### Lakelands

Wetlands are a striking feature of the Bréifne environment, the largest water bodies being Upper and Lower Lough Erne and Lough Allen. Ireland's two greatest rivers, the Shannon and the Erne, both rise in Cavan. Other principal lakes include Lough Melvin and to the north Lower and Upper Lough MacNean, with Lough Gill to the west and Lough Arrow and Lough Key at the southern end of the region. There are also numerous small lakes in the uplands and in the drumlin landscape of southern and eastern Bréifne. Lough Oughter, just north-west of Cavan town, is a complex of small inter-drumlin lakes connected by the meandering course of the River Erne.

Stands of reedbeds, wet grassland and wet woodland are found in the shallows and along the shores of many of the lakes. Some of the colourful plants visible

The Irish damselfly is a relatively uncommon species and was first discovered in Sligo in 1981. It has now been recorded at over 35 sites, many of them in Fermanagh
© Robert Thompson

## Animals

The otter is present throughout the waterways of Bréifne. It is primarily nocturnal and fish forms the main part of its diet.

The red squirrel is a native Irish species and feeds mainly on seeds and berries. It can be found in a range of habitats from coniferous forests to parklands.

The pine marten prefers deciduous woodlands and is generally active at night. It has a broad food diet and is an adept climber.

The common lizard is Ireland's only indigenous reptile species and is found on agricultural land, heath, beaches, dunes, meadows and bogs

Images ©Mike Brown

Reedbeds at Lough MacNean

are yellow water-lily, water mint, lesser spearwort and meadowsweet.

Many of the smaller lakes, with a well-developed fringe of emergent and swamp vegetation, are good areas for invertebrates, especially dragonflies, while the Irish damselfly is a speciality of Bréifne's drumlin country.

The lakes and their surrounding wetlands are important habitats for many species of birds. Common breeding species seen on lakes in Bréifne include tufted duck, moorhen, mute swan and the great crested grebe. In winter, many birds travel to the lakelands from Arctic regions. Large flocks of whooper swans from Iceland congregate and feed on the grasslands around the lakes, particularly Lough Erne and Lough Oughter.

### Coastline diversity

Bréifne's Atlantic coastline hosts a range of habitats – rocky seashores, tidal mudflats, salt marsh, sand dunes and grassland. From the coastline it is possible to spot whales and dolphins. Inishmurray Island, 6km offshore, is an important site for bird watching. Large numbers of eider duck are present as well as barnacle geese, shags, storm petrels and terns. Flowers, including

yellow iris and bluebells grow in abundance and there are profuse centaury blooms around August time. It's known as the 'Blessed Virgin flower', probably because of the Catholic feast of the Assumption which occurs on August 15.

Mullaghmore has an unusual habitat, a flat, grassy plain known as 'machair,' which is home to a mix of dry and wet loving plants. Machair is only found off the west coast of Ireland (Galway to Donegal) and the west coast of Scotland. The beautiful chough, a rare member of the crow family, is present along this coastline.

The tidal bays at Drumcliff and Sligo Harbour support large populations of waders, ducks and geese. In winter large numbers of barnacle geese can be witnessed making the journey south from Greenland. They can be seen feeding on the grassland at Lissadell. At low tide, groups of common seals lazing in their characteristic 'banana pose' can be seen on the sandbanks at Ballysadare.

Ballysadare Bay holds a large colony of common seals

## Valleys and lowlands

The valleys and lowlands are less ecologically interesting than the uplands, lakelands or the coast since they are primarily used for intensive farming. Most biodiversity interest in these areas is found in the waterways and small pockets of deciduous woodlands. Hedgerows, used as field boundaries, also serve an important role as wildlife corridors, linking discrete habitats. Given the scarcity of true woodland cover, hedgerows are also home to many woodland plants and animals. Along lowland river floodplains, such as stretches of the River Unshin and River Shannon, patches of reedbeds, fen and flooded alluvial woodland can still

### Flora

The strawberry tree grows around Lough Gill - its most northerly location in the world- and is more usally associated with Mediterranean regions

The hart's tongue fern is another habitat specialist and prefers the thin cracks and fissures of limestone pavement to put on its display

be found. Mammals such as otters are common and birds such as kingfishers may be glimpsed diving for a meal. One of the largest heronries in Ireland can be found at Crom, on the shores of Upper Lough Erne. Along fast-moving rocky stretches of river, birds such as grey wagtail and dipper can be seen. The Irish dipper is a unique race, having darker plumage than its British or continental cousins. Unlike birds such as the wagtail, which hunts insects from the air, the dipper walks underwater against the current to find its food, upturning rocks to look for insect larvae. At night, Daubenton's bat (one of seven species of bat recorded in Bréifne) hunts for insects above the rivers

and waterways. By day it roosts under old stone bridges.

Although it is a nationally scarce habitat, small areas of native deciduous woodland can still be found across Bréifne, with good examples at Cladagh Glen near Belcoo and Union Wood, south of Sligo. Mammals such as the elusive pine marten have been spotted in these woodland sites, while the red squirrel, which has not been ousted by the American grey squirrel, is still to be found in many similar places.

The type of deciduous woodland that develops in Bréifne is partly determined by the soil conditions. On dry, acid soils, sessile oak is

### Birds

1

2

4

The yellow iris is a wetland species found along lakeshores and marsh. It flowers from June to August. This habitat is comparatively species-rich

The milkwort is an upland species and prefers shallow peat where it can display its very unusual flower. It flowers from May to August

The gorse is very common in a range of habitats and its blossom makes an impressive display on the landscape in spring

the principal canopy tree. Below this, smaller trees such as holly and rowan form an understorey. Woodrush, hard fern and wood sorrel grow on the forest floor.

The humid, oceanic climate of Bréifne, particularly in its western half, allows the woodlands to support an abundance of mosses and liverworts. The climatic conditions also allow tiny filmy ferns to survive. On more fertile soils, ash and pedunculate oak form the canopy and there is a carpet of bluebells, wild garlic and wood anemone beneath. In wet sites alder, willow and birch are the main trees and the field layer contains plants suited to damp and sometimes flooded

conditions, including golden-leaved opposite saxifrage, remote sedge and yellow loosestrife which thrive on the forest floor.

The range of habitats in Bréifne provides extensive opportunities to get close to nature right throughout the year. Springtime brings the woodlands alive with birdsong and bluebells, while in summer the region is a feast of flowering plants and animals are at their most active. In autumn the bogs turn russet brown while in winter the lakes and coasts are host to flocks of wildfowl that have migrated from the Arctic.

The landscape upon which all this activity takes place can be enjoyed at any time.

The blackthorn blossom can be seen in most hedgerows and its blossom heralds the onset of spring

The primrose blossom is often seen in the woodlands and again is an early spring flowerer

1. The chough is the rarest member of crow family in Ireland and prefers rugged and undisturbed coastal cliffs and islands.

2. The eider is a sea duck and at Mullaghmore is at the southern limit of its European range. They gather in large groups inshore during the winter.

3. The kingfisher is one of Ireland's most beautiful birds and its preferred habitats are the larger, slow moving rivers in Bréifne.

4. The Arctic tern is a local summer visitor along the Sligo-Leitrim coastline. It winters from South Africa to the Antarctic.

5. The dipper's hunting technique is very unusual. Its name comes from its characteristic dipping action when standing.

Images 1, 2 © Irish Bird Images, 3,4,5 ©Mike Brown

Cutting turf in the traditional way

## Farming with Ignatius Maguire

Farming has always been a tradition and way of life in Bréifne. Its farmland was created by the retreat of the Ice Age and the influence of the large waterways, river systems and rolling upland areas which it left behind. While modern farming methods and agricultural industrialisation are omnipresent, the farm of Ignatius Maguire outside Belcoo remains one where the skills of farmers from another period are still cherished and practised.

Ignatius is the sixth generation of his family to have lived and worked this ground and he can trace his roots here as far back as 1740. The farm is outside Belcoo and looks west across Lattone Lough (Gaelic townland name meaning 'Half a Lake and Half a Hollow') towards Kiltyclogher, with Cuilcagh Mountain to its east.

The work is slower and less yielding than modern farming and follows a seasonal rhythm of rural life and change. Early spring sees the sowing of the potato plants, the barley crop and the eventual turning out of the dairy herd. Early summer sees the work of turf-cutting; mid summer the rhythmic use of the scythe in the meadow; late summer the drawing in of the hay and on to autumn, the time of harvest. The winning of the hay in July brings great satisfaction - a victory over the temperamental Irish climate and the winter feed won. Through it all continues a daily routine of milking, feeding and an intimate involvement with the countryside and all its treasures.

The eighth generation of the Maguires now lives on the Lattone holding. Watch and you may see the elusive hen harrier fly low over the land. Listen for the sounds of an idyllic countryside. Enjoy the wonderful sense of place and people. And Ignatius Maguire, at one with this wonderful place.

There is a sense of harmony and tradition on the farm

## Blanket bogs - a unique habitat

Peatlands once covered almost 20 per cent of the land area of Ireland - a higher proportion than any other European country except Finland. They are a unique habitat and their uniqueness can be compared to the semi-tropical and tropical rainforests in a number of remote regions in the world. The blanket bogs have traditionally been exploited as an indigenous fuel resource and as a building material. Heavy grazing has also had a debilitating influence. They are a seriously endangered western European habitat. Today turf cutting is restricted and, as they are some of the last remaining intact peatlands in Europe, Bréifne's blanket bogs are now protected by conservation legislation.

# SLIGO - MANORHAMILTON - DROMAHAIR

## Sligo

Sligo has always been considered the gateway from Connaught into Ulster and it rose to prominence with the Anglo-Norman invasion of Connaught in 1235. A castle was built in the town in 1245 and a Dominican friary in 1295. In 1310 a new castle and town were built by Richard III de Burgo, the Red Earl of Ulster, but the castle was destroyed in 1315. In the fifteenth and sixteenth centuries the town prospered, before being devastated in the wars against Queen Elizabeth I. It was captured by various forces during the seventeenth century, including Williamite rebels under Lord Kingston, and King James's men.

Sligo has a number of architecturally important late nineteenth-century buildings including the court house and the town hall. Today, it is the primary commercial, cultural

The Garavogue River runs through Sligo city

Sligo has a great range of pubs

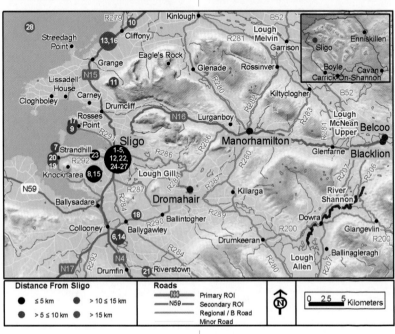

The wonderful produce from Cosgrove & Son in Sligo

and educational centre in Bréifne.

Sligo's Gaelic name, *Sligeach* (A Place Abounding in Shells), derives from the abundant shellfish found at the river and estuary. The city sits on the banks of the Garavogue River with Sligo Bay, Coolera Peninsula and the hill of Knocknarea to the west. Lough Gill is to the east, the ancient Ox Mountains to the south, and the limestone Dartry Mountains to the north.

The many cultural and tourist attractions include the sites that inspired Nobel prize-winning poet W B Yeats and his brother, artist Jack B Yeats. There are numerous theatres, art galleries, cinemas and entertainment for all the family. Nearby there are quality golf courses and opportunities for game and sea angling, diving, surfing, sailing, swimming, hill-walking, horse riding and a host of other leisure activities.

Sligo is very accessible with mainline rail and the N4 road network connections to Dublin. From Belfast and other main cities in Northern Ireland, the M1-A4-N16 routes provide easy access. It also has a

domestic airport with flights to and from Dublin and is 45 minutes from Knock Airport.

The Left Bank pub in Sligo

## Accommodation and eating out

Accommodation available in Sligo includes hotels, town and country homes, farm houses, guest houses, hostels, self-catering and caravan and camping. The main hotels include the four-star Clarion Hotel, the four-star Radisson SAS Hotel and Spa, the three-star Riverside Hotel, Sligo Park Hotel and the Sligo Southern Hotel. Top class entertainment and lifestyle extras such as gyms, swimming pools, saunas, hot tubs and health clubs are available.

Sligo has plenty of quality restaurants serving all types of cuisine. As well as those boasting talented chefs there are a good number of straightforward family-dining opportunities in the many restaurants, pubs, cafés and hotels in the city.

## Information points

1. **ℹ** Sligo Tourist Office and North West Tourism Temple Street
**T:** 00353 (0)71 9161201
**W:** irelandnorthwest.ie
**W:** sligotourism.ie
**Open:** All year

Dining options are extensive in Sligo and its hinterland

Evening strollers on Strandhill Beach

## 2. The Yeats Memorial Building
**T:** 00353 (0)71 9142693
**W:** yeats-sligo.com

[icons] Headquarters of the Yeats Society, the Yeats Memorial Building houses an exhibition on the poet and his family, and is also home to the Sligo Art Gallery. The famous Yeats International Summer School and Yeats Winter School are held here.

## 3. Cathedrals
[icon] It is worth visiting both of Sligo's cathedrals. The Cathedral of the Immaculate Conception is a Catholic cathedral first consecrated in 1874. It is famous for the lighting effect of 69 stained glass windows. The Cathedral of St John the Baptist, the Church of Ireland cathedral, was probably built on the site of an Anglo-Norman alms house. It dates from 1242. The famous German architect, Richard Cassels, redesigned it in 1730, but later Gothic features have replaced his work.

## 4. Sligo Abbey
**T:** 00353 (0)71 9146406
**Open:** March-October
[icons]

**The beautiful dining room at Markree Castle**

This is Sligo's only surviving medieval building and dates from 1252. Many of the tombs, monuments and features in this Dominican friary retain much of their original splendour. The abbey has had a chequered history, having been destroyed by fire in 1414 and gutted during the Tyrone War of 1595. It was also sacked and witnessed the massacre of its friars by Sir William Hamilton in 1642.

The eight lancet windows on the south side of the choir are from the thirteenth century. The sacristy and chapter house also date from the thirteenth century but the cloister and remaining buildings were added two centuries later. The abbey contains many fine tombs including the beautifully carved O'Crean tomb and the oldest decorated high altar in an Irish monastic church, dating probably to the fifteenth century. The abbey was also the burial place of many chieftains including Tighernan O' Rourke, King of Bréifne, who died in 1418.

## 5. The Green Fort
[icon] Behind the Model Arts and Niland Gallery and located above Connaughton Road is the Green Fort, a star-shaped earthwork artillery fortification, located on high ground to the north of the town and dating to around 1646. Sligo was extensively fortified during the Jacobite war and the Green Fort became the strongest part of its defences. After the Jacobite defeat at the Battle of the Boyne in July 1690, Sir Teige O'Regan took command of Sligo. He held out against constant attacks from the Williamites until September 1691, the Green Fort having at that time a Jacobite garrison of 600 men and 16 guns.

Sligo Abbey                    © Office of Public Works

## 6. Markree Castle

T: 00353 (0)71 9167800

Markree Castle, on the road from Collooney to Ballygawley, is surrounded by mature demesne woodland and the River Unshin runs through the grounds. Now a hotel, this seventeenth-century house has been home to the Cooper family since Cromwell's time. In 1832 Edward Cooper, an amateur astronomer, founded an important observatory there. The Markree telescope went to Hong Kong in 1932.

Jousting at the country fair in Markree Castle

## 7. Strandhill and Killaspugbrone Church

Strandhill's long stretches of strand are perfect for walking and surfing, though unsafe for bathing. North of Strandhill is the medieval Killaspugbrone Church built around the twelfth century. It is said that when St Patrick visited the church he fell and lost a tooth, which he gave to Bishop Bronus as a sign of friendship. The Fiacal Phadraig, (Shrine of St Patrick's Tooth), was created to house the holy tooth.

## 28. Inishmurray Island

Inishmurray Island is located about 6km off the coast of Sligo and contains some of the best preserved Early Christian remains in Ireland. It is also an internationally-important bird reserve and during the spring provides a truly memorable display of wildflowers.

The monastery was founded by St Molaise in the sixth century and was one of the first to be plundered by the Vikings in the eighth century. Three churches remain within the enclosure surrounded by 4m-high enclosed walls, the oldest of which, Teach Molaise, was probably the founder's tomb chapel. The Beehive Hut is referred to as the schoolhouse. Also within the enclosure are three altars, or *leachts*, with upright cross-engraved slabs. On one of these are the famous *Clocha Breaca* or Speckled Stones. When turned anti-clockwise they were used as cursing stones. The island also contains some 50 engraved stone slabs and pillars at which pilgrims recited the Stations of the Cross. Numerous artefacts have been discovered, including the wooden shrine of St Molaise, now in the National Museum.

The birdlife is notable for Arctic tern, storm petrel and barnacle geese. The island is also one of the most southerly nesting sites of the eider duck. Inishmurray remained inhabited until 1948, when the final 46 inhabitants left for the mainland.

Trips to the island take around an hour and a half each way and leave from Mullaghmore and Rosses Point. Visitors are advised to dress properly given the island's exposed location. Bring a packed lunch and observe best countryside practice when visiting this special place.

Images ©Office of Public Works

Inishmurray Island

The Beehive Hut

The enclosure

The schoolhouse

## 8. Carrowmore Passage Tomb Complex

**T**: 00353 (0)71 9161534
**Open**: Easter–October

🏃♿🏠€🅿🔋ℹ▶

Carrowmore, a megalithic cemetery, is one of the largest and most important collections of megalithic monuments in Europe, with a variety of chambered cairns, passage mounds, dolmens, standing stones and stone circles. The monuments form an oval-shaped cluster around a centrally-placed, cairn-covered monument, Listoghill (Tomb 51). Very early dates for some of the excavated tombs (4840– 4370 BC) remain debatable, but it is clear that these are among the oldest megalith tombs in Ireland, predating the Egyptian pyramids and also built some 700 years before

### Poets and revolutionaries

One of Ireland's leading poets, W B Yeats, is buried at Drumcliff near the Sligo coastline. Born in Dublin in 1865 he spent his early years between Dublin, London and Sligo. His first work *Mosada: A Dramatic Poem* was published in 1886, and there followed a series of famous works including *The Wind Among the Reeds* (1899), *The Green Helmet* (1910), *Easter 1916, The Wild Swans at Coole* (1919) and *Last Poems* (1939).

Yeats married George Hyde-Lees in 1917 and they had two children, Anne and Michael. His international reputation as a poet was assured from the 1920s and in 1923 he was awarded the Nobel Prize for Literature. The Irish State had already rewarded him with a seat in the Senate in 1922. He died on 28 January 1939 in Roquebrune, France and was buried there. In 1948 his remains were brought back to Ireland to rest, as he had wished, "under bare Ben Bulben's head" in Drumcliff churchyard.

Drumcliff church and its surrounding area was once an important ecclesiastical site. St Columba (also called Colmcille) founded a monastic settlement here in 574. Carvings on the well-known eleventh-century high cross in the graveyard of the church depict Adam and Eve, Daniel in the lion's den and the resurrection of Jesus.

The Gore-Booths lived at Lissadell House (see p14) near Drumcliff and the house has strong connections with the Yeats family also. Sir Robert Gore-Booth built Lissadell House in the 1830s. His son, Sir Henry, sailed to the rescue of the Arctic explorer, Leigh Smith, in 1882. In the next generation Sir Josslyn was a keen instigator of the co-operative movement and Eva was a noted suffragette.

Constance Gore-Booth (1868-1927), later known as Countess Markievicz, was born in 1868. She studied art in Paris, where she met and married a Polish count, Casimer de Markievicz. After her marriage she returned to Ireland. Her strong patriotic and nationalist views led her to fight in the Rebellion of 1916 as an officer of the Irish Citizen Army. She was sentenced to death but this was later commuted. The countess successfully contested the general election of 1918 and had the distinction of being the first woman to be elected to the British House of Commons, although she never took her seat. She was also Minister for Labour in the first Dáil Eireann and was re-elected to the Dáil in 1927 but died that year before taking her seat.

**Countess Markievicz in the uniform of the Irish Citizen Army**

Image ©National Museum of Ireland

**The graveyard at Drumcliff Church holds the remains of William Butler Yeats**

**The living room at Lissadell House**

## James Morrison

Sligo and Leitrim coastline offers good opportunities for surfing

Every year Riverstown hosts the James Morrison Traditional Music Festival in memory of the immensely talented fiddle player, who was born on 3 May 1893 at Drumfin, a townland on the Sligo-Dublin road near Collooney. The unique fiddle style which had emerged in Co Sligo around the late nineteenth century has had a major influence on Irish music right to the present day. James Morrison was foremost amongst the musicians who spearheaded this style of playing. Many tunes played by Irish musicians today are simply called 'Morrisons', an indication of the influence his records had on countless musicians over the years. James Morrison (or 'the professor') died in 1947 in New York.

Newgrange in Co Meath. A visitor centre operates during the summer period (see p70).

### 9. Rosses Point

This beautiful seaside village is set on a peninsula between the mountains of Ben Bulben and Knocknarea. Off the promenade is Oyster Island and beyond that Coney Island. In the middle of the channel stands the Metal Man, a gigantic statue of a seaman erected in 1822. His arm points to a place where the water is deep enough for ships.

### 10. Creevykeel Court Tomb

Creevykeel is one of the best examples of a court tomb in Ireland and dates from the Neolithic period 4000-2500BC. It has a cairn, entrance passage, an oval court and a double-chamber gallery. The cairn is wedge-shaped and the court is some 14m long. It was excavated in 1935 and this work uncovered four cremation burials, various items of Neolithic pottery, flint arrow heads, and other artefacts. The tomb is on the N15 Sligo to Bundoran road.

### 11. Ben Bulben

With sheer cliffs rising to a flat top, Ben Bulben (526m) is probably the most distinctive mountain in Ireland. The cliffs display the history of geological formation in the area and there are superb

### The Battle of the Books

Cooldrumman is located around the village of Carney, near Drumcliff and was the scene of a battle in 561, in what was probably the first ever copyright dispute. St Colmcille (also called St Columba) borrowed a famous psalter from St Finian and without his permission made a copy of it. Finian complained to the high king, who made probably the earliest copyright judgement: "To every cow its calf and to every book its copy." Colmcille and his followers took up arms against the ruling and the armies clashed at Cooldrumman where it is said that over 3,000 men were slain. As a penance St Colmcille was exiled and went to establish the great monastic settlement of Iona in Scotland.

The distinctive shape of the Glencar Valley and Ben Bulben

## Diarmuid and Gráinne

Fionn MacCumhail and Diarmuid Ó Duibhne, two legendary Irish figures, are associated with Ben Bulben. The story goes that Gráinne, a beautiful woman and daughter to the high king, was betrothed to Fionn, who was leader of the Fianna, an elite group of warriors. But she fell in love with Diarmuid, also a member of the Fianna, and forced him to elope with her.

Fionn's anger was such that he chased the couple all around Ireland. After many years, peace was made between Fionn and Diarmuid and the couple finally settled at Griannamore, a townland near Ballymote.

© Jim Fitzpatrick

One night at his new home Diarmuid was awakened by the sound of hounds barking and decided to investigate. He went to Ben Bulben, where Fionn and the Fianna were hunting. Fionn told Diarmuid that a wild boar had killed 50 of his men, and at that moment the huge boar appeared. Diarmuid plunged his sword into it, but before the mighty boar died it thrust its tusk into Diarmuid's side, fatally wounding him. As the hero lay dying he beseeched Fionn to use his magical healing powers to save his life by allowing him to drink water from his hands. Fionn collected water in his palms from a nearby spring, but, remembering the humiliation Diarmuid had caused him, let the water slip through his fingers. Fionn felt the cold stares of his men upon him and brought more water to the dying man. But he was too late. Before he could take a drink Diarmuid breathed his last on the side of Ben Bulben.

But Fionn's vengeance was only half realised. The leader of the Fianna sent Diarmuid's head to Gráinne, who died on seeing it. Diarmuid's friends carried her body to a cave and buried the couple together. This cave is known as Diarmuid and Gráinne's Cave and is located in the south-western corner of Gleniff Horseshoe Valley.

views on reaching the plateau, which is recognised as one of the most botanically-rich areas in Ireland. Hard limestone forms the upper cliffs and precipices while lower down are softer shales hidden beneath a scree formed of eroded fragments of Dartry limestone.

**12. Model Art and Niland Gallery**
T: 00353 (0)71 9141405
W: modelart.ie
Built as a 'model school' in 1882, the building has been redesigned and is now one of the premier arts centres in Ireland with an extensive programme of visual and performing arts. It is home to the Niland Art Collection, which features John and Jack B Yeats. Other local, national and international artists are also showcased in a contemporary exhibition programme. The performing arts programme includes contemporary music, comedy and drama, as well as classical concerts. There is also an award-winning gourmet café and a Black Box cinema programme. The local press and the gallery's website provide details on events and performances.

## Horse riding

Horse riding in Sligo offers a different perspective with the chance to experience the wildness and constantly changing landscape of Bréifne. There are headlong gallops in the white Atlantic foam and treks in the wilderness, uplands, forest trails, mountain paths and lakeshores. The Horse Holiday Farm, situated in the beautiful area of Green Island, directly on the Atlantic coastline, combines holidays and horses, while Markree Castle, a short distance from Sligo, offers a range of accommodation types, pony adventure camp, trails and bridle paths on its 350 year-old, 1,000-acre estate. The Sligo Riding Centre offers beginner to advanced outdoor rides and indoor lessons, as well as week-long trail rides and courses, while the family-run Island View centre provides riding lessons, treks and rides for all abilities, including riding holidays and clinics.

## Useful Contacts

**13. Horse Holiday Farm**
T: 00353 (0)71 9166152

**14. Markree Castle Riding Stables**
T: 00353 (0)71 9167800

**15. Sligo Riding Centre**
T: 00353 (0)71 9161353

**16. Island View Riding Stables**
T: 00353 (0)71 9166156

## Golf

**17/18/19.** There are several scenic 18 and nine-hole golf courses in Sligo. County Sligo Golf Club, better known as Rosses Point, has hosted many of Ireland's championships and has recently added a new nine-hole course. There is a new 18-hole championship golf course designed by Darren Clarke at Castledargan House in Ballygawley, while Strandhill Golf Course is a challenging links course. All local courses, including Ballymote Golf Club, host open competitions and 'classics' for visitors throughout the year.

**20. Celtic Seaweed Baths**
**T:** 00353 (0)71 9168686
**W:** celticseaweedbaths.com
The therapeutic benefit of seaweed baths is attributed to the high concentrations of iodine and trace minerals that occur naturally in seaweed and saltwater. Baths of hot saltwater and seaweed relieve aches and pains and replace vitamins and minerals. The seaweed is harvested locally and the bath is a great wellness tonic. Patrons have private rooms, each with their own cast iron bath and steam unit.

**21. Sligo Folk Park**
**T:** 00353 (0)71 9165001
**W:** sligofolkpark.com
**Open:** April-November
This community-based attraction depicts the experience of rural life and Irish heritage at the turn of the late nineteenth century. The museum has a great collection of rural history and agricultural artefacts. There is also a restaurant

**Seaweed baths are very therapeutic**

and pleasure grounds. Sligo Folk Park is located in the village of Riverstown, 24km from Sligo.

**22. Sligo Heritage and Genealogy Centre**
**T:** 00353 (0)71 9143728
The centre offers books on Sligo history and heritage, family crests and a full range of services to enquirers whose ancestors hail from Co Sligo.

**23. Woodville Farm**
**T:** 00353 (0)71 9162741
This is an historic working farm suitable for groups of all ages and interests, where visitors hold or feed the animals and collect eggs from the free-range hens. There is a farm machinery museum and guided tours are available. Pre-booking is essential.

**24. Sligo Regional Sports Centre**
The centre has a 25m indoor heated pool, children's pool, jacuzzi, sauna, steam room, air-conditioned fitness suite, large sports hall, spin-cycle studio and outdoor astro-turf pitch.

## Theatre and cinema

Theatre-goers are well catered for in Sligo. The Hawk's Well Theatre runs programmes of events including drama, music, opera and ballet involving national, international and community-based productions, while the Factory Theatre features productions by the Blue Raincoat Theatre Company, as well as invited national and international groups. The latter also hosts a three-week drama festival in the summer, daily lunchtime plays during the Yeats Summer School, and regular performances of world music or jazz.
The city centre 12-screen cinema has oversized screens and aircraft style seating.

**Sligo offers plenty of opportunity to enjoy the theatre**

### Useful Contacts

**24. Sligo Regional Sports Centre**
**T:** 00353 (0)71 9160539

**25. The Factory Theatre**
**T:** 00353 (0)71 9170431

**26. The Hawk's Well Theatre**
**T:** 00353 (0)71 9161518

**27. Sligo Gaiety Multiplex**
**T:** 00353 (0)71 9162651

Lough Arrow and Highwood under a shaft of light

# Manorhamilton

Manorhamilton was founded by Sir Frederick Hamilton, after he was granted 5,000 acres of land by King James I as part of the generally unsuccessful plantation of Leitrim. By 1631 he had increased his landholding to over 16,000 acres and in 1636 he built a fortified house, which gave the town its name. Much of his land previously belonged to the O'Rourkes who had been dispossessed following the defeat of the Irish chieftains at the 1601 Battle of Kinsale and the Flight of the Earls in 1607.

Sir Hamilton was reputed to have been extremely cruel, and in 1642 the Irish rebelled and burned the town. W B Yeats documented this cruelty in his short story *The Curse of the Fires and the Shadows*.

Manorhamilton was once the centre of the O'Rourkes' kingdom

By the middle of the eighteenth century the town had 233 houses. The Earl of Leitrim built a market-house in the centre of the town in 1834 and Manorhamilton courthouse was built the following year. During the early days of the Great Famine, a workhouse was built. This was demolished and replaced by a hospital in 1954.

Manorhamilton lies in the centre of the North Leitrim Glens and is surrounded by the Ben Bulben-Tievebaun Mountains, Arroo Mountain and the Boleybrack uplands. Its Gaelic name is *Cluainin* (Little Meadow) and dates to when the powerful O'Rourke clan ruled the area. This picturesque town is thriving and expanding. Its country market is held every

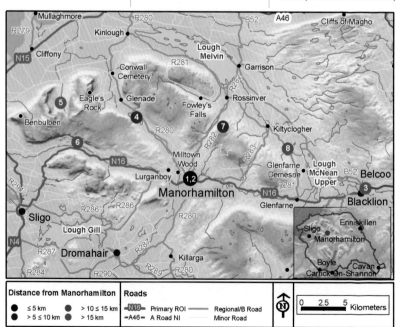

| Distance from Manorhamilton | Roads | | |
|---|---|---|---|
| ● ≤5 km  ● >10 ≤ 15 km | N16 Primary ROI | Regional/B Road | |
| ● >5 ≤ 10 km  ● > 15 km | A46 A Road NI | Minor Road | |

0  2.5  5 Kilometers

Manorhamilton Castle is a fortified house of the type popular with seventeenth century planters

Friday and there is a large annual agricultural show held in July. Manorhamilton offers activities such as golfing, walking, angling, potholing and caving. The area surrounding the town is also rich in heritage and natural beauty. At least two of W B Yeats' poems relate to the area and its history. Manothamilton is 26 km from Sligo and 28 km from Enniskillen and is in the heart of the Bréifne region.

## Accommodation and eating out

Manorhamilton and the immediate surrounding areas provide accommodation in the form of guesthouses, hostels and a good selection of welcoming B&Bs. There is a variety of restaurants, cafés and pubs in the area.

### 1. The Glens Centre
**T:** 00353 (0)71 9855833
**W:** theglenscentre.com
The Glens Centre theatrical performance and cultural facility is located in a converted Methodist church in Manorhamilton that

The Sculpture Centre

dates back to the 1820s. The intimate theatre has tiered seating for up to 140 and provides quality entertainment throughout the year. The centre also houses rehearsal space, recording facilities and self-catering apartments. The centre organises hill-walking festivals at Easter, August and October holiday weekends. Check the local papers for the wide range of music, poetry, plays and storytelling on offer.

### 2. Leitrim Sculpture Centre
**T:** 00353 (0)71 9855833
This centre houses high quality exhibitions and works of art, and also offers courses and training to students from Ireland and abroad. Its founding members included a number of locally based artists of national and international repute working in stone, wood and bronze.

### 3. Lough MacNean Sculpture Trail
The Lough MacNean Sculpture Trail is set in a landscape of outstanding natural beauty around the shores of Upper and Lower Lough MacNean, in south-west Fermanagh and

Manorhamilton Agricultural Fair

bordering with counties Cavan and Leitrim. Amid this setting 11 pieces of sculpture have been placed on sites that vary from a wooded river glen to the grounds of a large eighteenth-century estate and lakeside forest park. Each sculpture is the result of ten weeks' work by an artist, and reflects collaboration with local communities, youth groups and schools.

### 4. Glenade Lake and Eagles Rock

This wild and rugged district makes for excellent scenic driving. Glenade is an example of one of Bréifne's glacial valleys and contains the spectacular sight of Eagle's Rock, a free-standing slab of limestone that has slipped away from the cliff after the retreat of the ice that once supported it. The lake is home to rare aquatic plants such as quillwort and slender naiad, which are testimony to its good water quality.

### 5. Gleniff Horseshoe

Gleniff Horseshoe is a spectacular scenic route through one of the most botanically-rich areas in Ireland. The horseshoe shaped-drive, east of Grange and south-west of Kinlough, provides impressive views of dramatic scenery and wild mountains, including the prominent wave-shaped Benwiskin. At the head of the valley the sheer limestone cliffs form a huge amphitheatre, and the cliffs provide examples of arctic-alpine vegetation, including some species found nowhere else in Ireland.

Glencar Waterfall

### 6. Glencar Waterfall and Valley

The 17m waterfall that tumbles in the Glencar Valley beauty spot was immortalised by W B Yeats in his poem 'The Stolen Child'. The waterfall is impressive and can be viewed from a lovely wooded walk. Picnic facilities are also provided. Glencar itself is a classic example of a U-shaped valley, carved by a glacier.

### 7. Lisdarush Hillfort

There are wonderful views from Lisdarush Hillfort, which is thought to date from around 450. It is strategically located overlooking the junction of two river valleys connecting Lough Melvin with the area around Manorhamilton. It is a grass-covered circular area defined by an earthen bank, a ditch and second bank. Hill forts may have been used for specific rituals and seasonal gatherings. The site has never been excavated and can be found on the road between Manorhamilton and Rossinver.

### 8. Prince Conall's Grave

Prince Conall's Grave is an interesting megalithic tomb, located on the Glenfarne to Kiltyclogher road. It has been described

## The legend of the dobhar-chú

Dobhar-chú or 'water hound' is the Gaelic word for otter. The legend tells of Grace Connelly who lived near Glenade at the beginning of the eighteenth century. When washing clothes at the lake, she was attacked and killed by the dobhar-chú. Her husband found her body lying by the lakeside with the creature lying asleep on her breast. He crept up on the dobhar-chú and killed it. The dying creature cried out in agony and a similar beast sprang out of the lake and chased the man across the country as far as Cashelgarron. When the man's horse became exhausted and lay down, the avenging dobhar-chú pierced the horse with its horn. The man seized this opportunity to kill the creature by stabbing it through its heart.

Conwell Cemetery at Glenade, on the road between Manorhamilton and Kinlough, holds a recumbent gravestone which echoes the legend. Situated in the middle of the cemetery, the gravestone has, at its top right hand corner, an image of a dog-like creature being stabbed by a human hand. Barely legible on the tombstone are the words: ...ODY OF GRACE CONN/Y WIFE TO TER MACLOGHLIN WHO DYD 7BER THE 24TH ANN DMI MDCCXXII.

## The Organic Centre

**T:** 00353 (0)71 9854338   **W:** theorganiccentre.ie

Located a couple of kilometres from Rossinver, the Organic Centre is Ireland's leading centre devoted to the teaching of organic gardening, growing and farming. Encompassing 19 acres, the centre offers a range of specific themed gardens, including demonstration, children's, heritage, taste, kitchen, unusual vegetables and salad gardens. Other features include a composting techniques display, a willow sculpture area, an orchard and soft fruit area and a café (open in the summer months). A shop stocks herbs, transplants, organic compost, books, seeds and tools.

as a court tomb, wedge tomb and even as a passage tomb. However, it does not fit within any simple classification and in some ways is a unique monument type. It consists of a D-shaped cairn defined by upright stones and dry-stone walling, containing a single megalithic chamber with a displaced roofslab. The entrance stone is not set in the ground and it is this stone, with its kennel-hole entrance, that makes the monument unique. The site was reconstructed somewhat in 1953 following an excavation, which uncovered Neolithic hollow scrapers, thumb-nail scrapers, a leaf-shaped arrowhead and some coarse pottery.

### Fishing and festivals

The plentiful rivers and lakes around Manorhamilton are an angler's paradise with salmon, sea trout, ferox, gilleroo, sonaghan, char, eel, perch, bream, roach and pike. Upper Lough MacNean has a fishing stand adapted for disabled anglers. Permits and all equipment can be obtained locally (see p146). Glenfarne village hosts the Glenfarne Gala weekend festival in the summer. The Glens Centre organises hill-walking festivals that cater for all levels of fitness.

### Walking and potholing

From Rossinver there is a good short walk along the river to Fowley's Falls and there are woodland trails at Milltown Wood and Glenfarne Demesne. The surrounding hills of Manorhamilton provide walking opportunities on both sides of the border, as well as potholing opportunities in the extensive underground cave systems. (See page 152)

Prince Conall's grave

## The skill of the thatcher

**Hughie Cullen**

The thatched cottage is an iconic image of old Ireland and one with which most visitors are familiar. While housing styles nowadays are very different to yesteryear, the skill of thatching is still very much admired and appreciated.

Hughie Cullen is a native of Kiltyclogher and has mastered the skills of this unique craft over many years. The tools of his trade are remarkably simple - straw, a wooden mallet, a ladder, a knife, willow rods and bent wooden staples or scallops. From this the expert thatcher can construct a roof that will last between eight and 20 years depending on the choice of straw.

The traditional choice was to use only local and indigenous materials such as the straw of wheat, oats, barley and rye. For most of Ireland the thatching style was known as 'pinned thatch' in which the straw was held in place using wooden pins or scallops. Modern farming methods have meant that the traditional long straw is no longer available and has to be specially grown with the result that a lot of the straw now comes from Poland and Eastern Europe.

Once a prominent feature on the landscape, thatched houses are now much less numerous. They still are, however, a unique and beautiful part of the landscape and heritage of Bréifne. Hughie Cullen keeps both the craft and the vernacular thatched house style alive. To appreciate the craft of thatching and the work of Hughie Cullen, visit the thatched family homestead of the late Seán Mac Diarmada near Kiltyclogher.

The craftsman at work

The pinned thatching style which uses wooden scallops is the most common

Outdoor cooking at Markree Castle summer festival

## The Ballroom of Romance

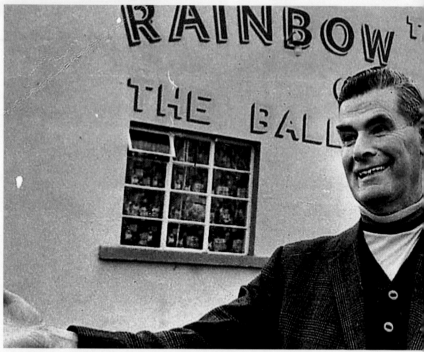

John McGivern, the founder of the Ballrroom of Romance

The English writer, William Trevor, made the locally renowned dance-hall in Glenfarne famous to a world audience when he wrote his book *The Ballroom of Romance* in the 1970s. Passing through Glenfarne, the writer noticed a hall with 'Ballroom of Romance' written on the front wall. He was intrigued, and upon making some enquiries decided to write his book. The BBC made a film based on the book and it was acclaimed internationally.

The dance-hall was built by the late John McGivern in early 1934 and was known then as McGivern's Dance Hall. The opening function consisted of a variety concert followed by the first dance in the new hall with music by the Glenfarne Dance Band.
Over the next two decades the hall went from strength to

strength and in 1952 John decided to extend it. A few years afterwards rural electricity and piped water became available to replace tilly lamps and chemical toilets. This served to make the extended hall much more modern and the Rainbow continued to attract large numbers from all over the country. When John re-opened the hall after the 1952 renovations he renamed it 'The Rainbow Ballroom of Romance.'

During the great years of the showband era in Ireland, from the mid 1950s to the early 1980,s all the top Irish bands played in the Rainbow. Bands such as Hugh Toorish and the famous Clipper Carlton from Strabane were regular performers. Other bands appearing regularly included Brendan Boyer and the Royal, Dickie Rock and the Miami, Joe

McCarthy and the Dixies, Sean Fagan, Sonny Knowles and the Pacific, Big Tom and the Mainliners, Susan McCann, Philomena Begley, Joe Dolan, Brian Coll and the Buckaroos and many more. One of the most popular bands with the Rainbow patrons was the great Melody Aces from Newtownstewart.

Local bands also played in the Rainbow: the Bréifne Dance Band from Glenfarne, The Emerald Valley Band from Rossinver, The Rhythm Swing from Glencar, Kevin Wood's Band from Drumshambo, Frank Murray's band from Carrick-on-Shannon, The Starlight band from Derrylin, The Red Sunbeam from Swanlinbar, Pat O'Hara and his band from Strandhill, and many others. Many top groups and solo performers from Ireland and abroad also played in concert

at the Rainbow: The Dubliners, Foster and Allen, The Dublin City Ramblers, The Wolfe Tones, Anna McGoldrick, Joe Lynch, Ruby Murray, Bridie Gallagher, Daniel O'Donnell, Eileen Donaghy, Altan, the Gallowglass Ceili Band and many more. Also from abroad came the Harry Gold Orchestra, Ronnie Ronald, Victor Sylvester Big Band, and Scotland's favourite, the Jimmy Shand Ceili Band.

At the dances John would introduce what he called 'the romantic interlude'. This involved John joining the band for 15 to 20 minutes on stage, dressed in a black suit, white shirt and black bow-tie, to sing such romantic songs as 'Have You Ever Been Lonely', the popular Jim Reeves song 'He'll Have To Go' and others. John would ask the dancing couples to get to know each other by shaking hands and exchanging greetings. He would also give out spot-prizes to lucky couples, usually tickets for future dances. During his romantic interludes the hall lights would be dimmed and the men would be encouraged to take their lady to the bar for a cup of tea or a mineral drink (no alcohol in those days). A lot of happy marriages resulted from meetings at these interludes and this was what inspired John to add 'The Ballroom of Romance' to the name of the hall.

The Glenfarne Community Development Trust, who now lease the hall, organise many types of functions such as ceilis, dancing classes, concerts, acting workshops, music classes, fundraising auctions and sales. It could be said that once again the Rainbow is at the heart of the community in Glenfarne and its surroundings.

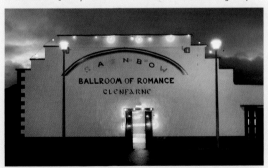

Glenfarne's Ballroom of Romance has a special place in the social history of the region

## Lough Gill

One of Ireland's most beautiful lakes, the naturally nutrient rich Lough Gill is about 10km long and 3km wide and mute swan, cormorant, gulls, ducks and heron can all be seen. It is home to Parke's Castle and Innisfree Island, immortalised in one of WB Yeats most famous poems. The woodlands around the lake are some of the best examples of semi-natural deciduous woodland in Bréifne with a great diversity of flora and fauna. Interesting locations around the lake include Tobernalt Holy Well and Slish Wood, referred to by Yeats in his poem

# Dromahair

The area around Dromahair was the seat of the O'Rourkes, who were the dominant family in this part of Bréifne for centuries. In 1628, as part of the Plantation of Ulster, Sir William Villiers was granted land in the area. He built Dromahair Castle, known locally as Villier's Castle, and began the task of establishing a town. The town was substantially improved in the nineteenth century through the patronage of the landowner at the time, Mr Lane Fox. Situated on the banks of the River Bonet near its entry point to Lough Gill, Dromahair's Gaelic name is *Droim Dhá Thiar*, which is locally translated as the Ridge of Two Demons, however, the actual meaning of the last word is uncertain. The landscape is varied,

combining upland, lakeland and lowland. The Ox Mountains run through the area and north of these lies Lough Gill while on its northern shore are the uplands of the Crockauns and Doons. To the south, Dromahair itself sits in a lowland area.

This small town and its surroundings have interesting history and archaeology and many come to visit places such as Innisfree and Dooney Rock, made famous by Ireland's most celebrated poet, W B Yeats. Salmon and trout fishing, as well as Parke's Castle and the Ard Nahoo Health Farm are also close at hand. Traditional musicians and followers will be attracted to nearby Riverstown, which holds an annual festival in honour of the renowned fiddle player James Morrison.

Dromahair is only 20km from Sligo and 55km from Enniskillen.

Farmers markets and country fairs are popular during the summer

## Accommodation and eating out

Holiday cottages and farm accommodation are available in and around Dromahair. The Breffni Cottages are located on the banks of the River Bonet while the Abbey Hotel has 26 bedrooms and is central to the town. It also provides

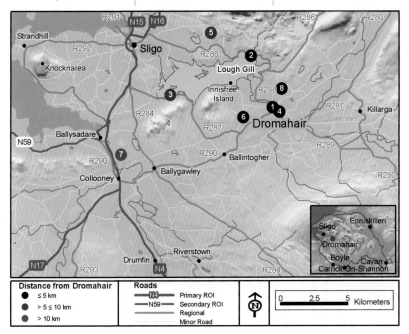

Distance from Dromahair
● ≤ 5 km
● > 5 ≤ 10 km
● > 10 km

Roads
━N4━ Primary ROI
━N59━ Secondary ROI
Regional
Minor Road

0   2.5   5 Kilometers

A group session at the James Morrison Festival

An exhibit at the Steam Rally in Riverstown

self-catering apartments and townhouses in a restored mill and railway buildings along the river. Markree Castle near Collooney also has great accommodation and wonderful grounds. Places to eat in Dromahair include the Abbey Manor Hotel and Stanford's Village Inn, which serves light pub fare.

## Information point

**Leitrim Tourist Office**
Old Barrell Store
Carrick-on-Shannon
**T:** 00353 (0)71 9620170
**W:** www.leitrimtourism.com
**Open:** Seasonal

### 1. Creevelea Friary
A ten-minute walk from Dromahair along the River Bonnet leads to the preserved remains of this Franciscan friary, founded in 1508. It stands beside the river and the friary consists of the church, with a beautiful arched window, a cloister, the arcading of which contains two carvings of St Francis, and domestic buildings. The friary had a short and turbulent history. It was partly destroyed by fire in 1536, then suppressed under Henry VIII.

### 2. Innisfree Island and Parke's Castle
*I will arise and go now, and go to Innisfree...* Depart from Parke's Castle in Leitrim (or Doorly Park in Sligo) to visit this island made famous by W B Yeats and take the leisurely cruise across Lough Gill for a trip in an area of outstanding natural beauty, steeped in myth and legend. Live commentary and poetry recitals are part of the experience. Parke's Castle, an impressive manor house, sits on the shores Lough Gill. Its splendour (see p79) is evident when cruising around the lake. There are guided tours of the castle every hour as well as an audio-visual slide show in four languages.

### 3. Dooney Rock
W B Yeats' poem 'The Fiddler of Dooney' has made this beauty spot famous. A walk along the woodland trail runs near to where gneiss rock from the Ox Mountains, dating back 750 million years, meets the much younger limestone.
*When I play on my fiddle at Dooney,*
*Folk dance like a wave on the sea.*

### 4. Dromahair Castle
Dromahair Castle is a fortified house, probably constructed in the early seventeenth century by Sir William Villiers. The O'Rourkes are often mistakenly credited with the construction of this castle, perhaps because of its proximity to O'Rourkes Hall. The house, which is U-shaped and three storeys high, consists of a main

Creevelea Friary was finally abandoned by the friars at the end of the seventeenth century
Image © Office of Public Works

block with two wings. It is surrounded by a rectangular bawn or courtyard, defined by a stone wall.

### 5. Deerpark Forest and Court Tomb

A number of trails go through the state-owned forest but the main attraction is the tomb of Magheraghanrush, which dates to the Neolithic period. Its most distinctive feature is the open court at the centre, which was used for ritual and provided access to three galleries. Large lintel stones once spanned the entrances to the galleries but only one survives. In the nineteenth century, exploratory excavations uncovered human and animal bones.

### 6. Killerry Church

The church is a simple stone structure with a large east window but is worth a visit for the 'straining stones' in its cemetery. These are seven egg-shaped stones set around a small rectangular stone with pieces of string tied around them. This 'straining string' supposedly possesses an infallible cure for all manner of aches and strains. The ritual involves removing a piece of string from a 'straining stone' and replacing it with another string. Then prayers are said as each stone is turned. The egg-shaped stones are typical of what are known as 'praying stones', a feature of Early Christian sites.

### 7. Union Wood

Union Wood, south of Lough Gill, is one of the best remaining examples of old oak woodland in Bréifne and is home to a number of mammals species including

badger, deer, fox, red squirrel and the rare pine marten. The abundance of mosses and ferns is characteristic of woods in western Ireland due to the mild and wet oceanic climate. There are a series of forest walks to be enjoyed and one of these links with the Sligo Way. Car parking is provided.

### 8. Ard Nahoo Health Farm

**T:** 00353 (0)71 9134939
**W:** www.ardnahoo.com

A short distance from Dromahair and a million miles from the stresses of modern living, Ard Nahoo overlooks Loch Nahoo in a place of great natural beauty. Aside from the extensive programme of therapies, massage and health treatment packages, Ard Nahoo also appeals to the 'green tourist' wanting to explore the North Leitrim Glens. Guests stay in cosy log cabins fully equipped for self-catering. The health farm also runs courses in yoga, meditation, reiki, detoxification and vegetarian whole-food cooking.

Wellness therapy at Ard Nahoo Health Farm

## The O'Rourkes

The O'Rourkes were descendants of the Ui Briuin, a tribe that inhabited the central area of Connaught during the fifth and sixth centuries. In the eighth century a section of this kin-group broke away and entered the area of Bréifne where they became known as the Ui Briuin Bréifne. The name O'Rourke (Ua Ruairc) was first used as a surname in the tenth century when Fergal, the chief of Bréifne, took his grandfather's name, Ruarc.

For the next 650 years the O'Rourkes were the ruling power in Bréifne, though they became confined to west Bréifne in the thirteenth century when the O'Reillys gained control over east Bréifne. In the twelfth century, the O'Rourke chiefs, from Fearghal down to Tighearnán Mór, were preoccupied with the twin objectives of becoming kings of Connaught and conquering Meath. Indeed in the tenth and eleventh centuries, the O'Rourkes provided four kings of Connaught.

In the first half of the seventeenth century the O'Rourke kingdom of west Bréifne was coveted by the O'Donnells and O'Neills of Ulster who saw it as a buffer on their western border. The English government also saw that a west Bréifne loyal to the Crown would be advantageous to their plans to consolidate their hold on Connaught. This left the O'Rourkes in an almost impossible situation and by 1661 they had been completely dispossessed and their lands planted with English settlers.

Teenagers enjoy canoeing on Lough Allen

# SPECIAL INTERESTS AND ACTIVITIES

Fishing

Cruising

Walking and cycling

Water sports

Traditional music

Crafts

Railways

The large network of lakes and river systems offers Ireland's best game and coarse angling

# FISHING

Bréifne is Ireland's premier location for game and coarse fishing and has some of the cleanest and most lightly fished fresh waters in Europe. The country's two great rivers, the Shannon and the Erne, both rise in the drumlin county of Cavan. Their massive lake and river systems provide great opportunities for top class angling. The concentration and variety of accessible mixed fishing has attracted anglers from all around the world for many years.

The lake systems of Lough Erne, Lough Melvin, Lough Gill, Lough Allen and Lough Key provide excellent mayfly, trout and salmon fishing. The Upper Erne, Annalee and Lough Oughter lake systems are noteworthy for regular specimen catches of bream, tench, pike and rudd. For the sea angler there is shore, beach and rock fishing along the Sligo coast. Hired boats are also available for deep-sea angling.

Salmon runs are found on Loughs Melvin and Gill and in the Glencar Valley, while the Ballisodare River at Collooney is recognised for its prolific salmon catches. People fishing for trout can also enjoy wet fly on those lakes, while Lough Key, Lough Gill and Lough Erne are all particularly suitable for the dry fly. Lough Arrow, where the late John Henderson and his son pioneered the art of dry fly fishing from 1900 onwards is a particular favourite. All these lakes also have good mayfly hatches and all contain large ferox type trout with catches featuring between 7lb and 17lb.

Most of the lakes of Cavan and Leitrim hold pike to specimen size. Notable for larger specimens are Temple House Lake, Ballymote, Lough Key and Lough Garra. The Erne system and Lough MacNean are good also for pike. Specimens between 20lb and 40lb have been recorded. The lake systems around Ballinamore have recently seen the Irish record bream catch broken –

the record had stood for over 100 years. Lough Melvin holds three genetically distinct trout types – the sonaghan, ferox and gillaroo and these offer deep lake, trolling and rocky shore challenges

A 20lb pike caught in Bunn Lake, Cavan

## Sea angling in Bréifne

The Bréifne coastline, over 153km long, has some of the cleanest and clearest waters in Europe. It is also one of the most varied, with dramatic cliffs, white surf, rugged rocky coastline and large expanses of pale sands. The North Atlantic Drift effect on Ireland's west coast keeps Bréifne sea waters temperate. For this

**Two beautiful tench caught on Colga Lake, Leitrim**

Fishermen will find Gabriel Owens, owner of the Forge Tackle Shop in Ballinamore, a source of great information on the area's fishing

reason, unusual warm water species such as triggerfish, red bream and amberjack often turn up in catches here. Numerous sea angling competitions are fished annually and, in recent years, up to 34 species of fish have been recorded. Shore angling is becoming increasingly popular with fishing carried out from numerous shores, beaches and piers. The best stands are sign-posted. Chartered sea angling boat trips are available along the Bréifne coast. Equipment hire is also available.

## Safety

All vessels should carry the correct licence documentation on board and you are advised to confirm with the operator of the vessel that they are fully licensed and approved by the relevant authority. Remember to wear life jackets and suitable all-weather clothing. Chest waders are recommended for river fishing. It is always advisable to tell someone your anticipated return time.

## Fishing licences

In the Republic of Ireland you do not need a licence to fish for trout, coarse species or in the sea. However, if you intend to fish for salmon or sea trout you must have a State Salmon and Sea Trout Fishing Licence, available as a national licence or a district licence. A national licence covers all fishery board districts while a district licence covers only the fishery district in which the licence is purchased. These licences can be purchased from select fishing tackle shops. The fishing tackle shops listed sell the appropriate licence. Alternatively, licences can be bought online on the Central Fisheries Board website at www.cfb.ie. In Northern Ireland the responsible authority is the Fisheries Conservancy Board for Northern Ireland (www.fcbni.com). Licences and permits where required can be purchased from it, or one of the many licence and permit distributors.

## Share certificates

Separate to licence and permit requirements are share certificates. There are eight fisheries development societies in Ireland. Their purpose is to raise funds for the development of coarse and trout fishing. At present the Northern Fisheries Development Society (Northern Fisheries Region) is the only area in the country where a share certificate is required in order to fish. Consult the Central Fisheries Board website at www.cfb.ie for all information relating to fishing in Ireland.

(See pages 26 and 169)

Ground bait, maggots and accessories are available in many of the area's angling centres

The day's sea angling catch

# CRUISING

Three navigable waterways traverse Bréifne - the Shannon and Erne Rivers and the Shannon-Erne Canal. Cruising is a very popular activity in the region and cruisers and barges of all sizes can be hired in Carrick-on-Shannon, Belturbet, Ballinamore, Derrylin and Belleek.

Boats usually cater for between two and 10 people. No specialist knowledge is needed to hire a cruiser and no licence is required. The cruiser company will demonstrate the fundamentals when you arrive to pick up the boat. Navigational charts and a captain's handbook are supplied. It is imperative to observe at all times the personal safety recommendations and provisions.

An alternative to the cruiser is the traditional wide-beamed barge and these are available for hire at Ballinamore and Derrylin. Rental periods are usually from Saturday to Saturday although some companies offer shorter rental periods for short breaks. Costs vary depending on season, size and specification of boat. The cruise company usually requires a 25 per cent deposit upon booking and you must be at least 21 years old to hire the vessel.

The River Erne is navigable from Belleek in Co Fermanagh to Belturbet in Co Cavan. There is only one lock on the Erne. Pump-outs and toilet facilities are located at Belleek, Enniskillen, Galloon and Knockninny. Other slipways and jetties are located in Enniskillen, Bellanaleck and at numerous other locations on the river.

Reopened in 1994, the Shannon-Erne Waterway links the rivers Shannon and Erne, creating over 300km of navigable waters and Europe's longest navigable inland stretch. The scenic Shannon-Erne link features 16 fully automated locks, 34 stone bridges and six fully serviced mooring areas. The service areas are located at Keshcarrigan, Leitrim village, Ballinamore, Haughton's

Pleasure craft of all sorts can be hired at a number of locations around the waterways

**The marina at Ballyconnell**

Shore, Ballyconnell and Aghalane. Facilities provided for waterway users at these locations include toilets, showers, pump-outs and laundry facilities.

Lough Allen and its mooring and picnic areas can be accessed by turning right off the Shannon-Erne canal onto the Lough Allen Canal just below Leitrim village. Cruise through Acres Lake at Drumshanbo and into Lough Allen. The Acres Lake amenity area provides waterside leisure facilities,

including mooring area, heated swimming pool, angling jetty, tennis courts and children's play area. Spencer Harbour on the northern shore of Lough Allen and Cleighan Mór near Ballinagleragh on the eastern shore are also mooring areas and worth a visit.

Services on the Shannon are located in Leitrim village, Drumshanbo, Dromod, Drumsna, Carrick-on-Shannon, Lough Allen and Ballyleague.

As with all activities on water, safety is a paramount concern and your boat hire provider should provide details on proper safety procedures. Always use up-to-date navigation maps for the waterway you are on and follow the navigation marks on rivers and lakes. Listen to the local weather forecasts and notify someone of your expected time of arrival before setting out. It is important to also respect the wildlife of the waterways and be mindful that the boat wash can cause serious disruption to bank-side nesting sites.

One of the advantages of cruising in Bréifne is travelling at your own pace. The waters are among the least congested in Europe. The towns and villages provide plenty of restaurants and pubs at which to stop and enjoy a hearty meal or drink. The network of waterways offers some of Europe's finest opportunities to enjoy this unique type of holiday experience.

**Carrick-on-Shannon, a gateway location from which to explore the waterways of Bréifne**

The cosy interior of the barge

The mooring in Ballinamore

# WALKING AND CYCLING

The varied landscapes of Bréifne offer a large selection of walking choices for both the leisurely stroller and the more committed walker. With mountain ranges, upland areas and the quiet open countryside it is possible to find a route to suit all abilities.

There are four 'waymarked ways' in Bréifne. These do not demand great stamina, difficult navigation or climbing techniques. The routes wind through beautiful countryside taking in aspects of Bréifne which otherwise might be missed. The ways themselves are signposted with standard markers: the yellow arrow and walking man will guide you. A grading system for these walks is available for each section. This is based on a number of indicators including underfoot conditions, quality of marking and trail furniture. Trails can be 'easy', 'medium' or 'hard'. Maps and details of walks can be downloaded from the Bréifne website (www.breifne.ie).

## The Ulster Way

The Ulster Way is a 900km footpath encircling Northern Ireland of which 160km goes through Co Fermanagh and the towns of Pettigo, Belcoo, over Cuilcagh Mountain, Florencecourt, Derrylin and Lisnaskea. The Ulster Way travels through forests, over mountains and provides some stunning views. The entire route is signposted, but a good map is desirable.

## Slí Cabháin (The Cavan Way)

The Cavan Way marked trail runs between Dowra and Blacklion, where it links with the Ulster Way. The route covers 26km of undulating Cavan landscape which has lots of archaeological features and is rich in folklore. The trail takes the walker past the Shannon Pot and most of the walking terrain is on quiet roads. This is ideal for a one or two-day walk.

## Sliabh an Iarainn (The Iron Mountain)

This is a 20km walk on country roads, through forestry and on open mountain. It is on the eastern shore of Lough Allen and crests at 585m. The mountain takes it name from the iron deposits found in the rocks in this area.

The walker's panoramic view from the summit of Cuilcagh Mountain

Camping along the shores of Devenish Island

## Slí Liatroma (The Leitrim Way)

This 48km walk begins in Drumshanbo and Manorhamilton and traverses drumlin country with hedgerows and wild flowers. The route also offers splendid mountain and lake views. Ideal for a one or two-day walk.

## Slí Shligeach (The Sligo Way)

Following the line of the Ox Mountains, this 74km walk begins at Lough Talt on the Sligo-Mayo border and progresses to Dromahair at the south-east end of Lough Gill. Approximately 21km of the Sligo Way is in the region, again representing a one to two-day walk.

## Cuilcagh Way Walking Route

There are six options in this route which is part of the Ulster Waymarked Way and all offer a different experience. The Cladagh Glen is a 3.3km walk with its highest point at 175m; the Cuilcagh Mountain Park walk is 4.2km and peaks at 395m; the Legnabrocky Track on Cuilcagh Mountain is 7.2km long and, at 665m,

is the highest walk; Legacurragh Valley is 6.7km and 310m high while Florencecourt Forest is 7.2km and 270m high; the final way is Gortmaconnell Rock at 4.7km long and 195m high. All are well signposted and offer a great choice in an area of outstanding beauty.

## Miner's Way and Historical Trail

The Miner's Way and Historical Trail are both waymarked long-distance walking routes that form a network of paths in counties Leitrim, Roscommon and Sligo. Beginning in Arigna, the path meanders through the coal mining territory of the Arigna Mountains, tracing the routes followed by the miners going to their work. The trail then goes westward through Lough Key Forest Park in Boyle. This part of the walk is known as the Historical Trail. The walk goes on to cross the Curlew and Bricklieve Mountains and through Castlebaldwin before rejoining the Miner's Way at Ballyfarnon. The walks total 118km, with the highest point being the Curlew Mountains (250m). This walk can be broken

down into smaller sections for ease.

## Town trails

Of the five main centres of population in the region Sligo, Enniskillen and Carrick-On-Shannon have gentle walking tours through the towns. These will inform and direct you through the town pointing out places of interest.

## Other walks and trails

Aside from the waymarked ways there are plenty of other walks and trails including waterway and

Proper footware is important for those out walking

heritage walks and lots of lakeside and forest trails. These include Lough Navar Forest near Derrygonnelly, Lough Key Forest Park near Boyle, Killykeen Forest Park outside Cavan and the North Leitrim Glens. Information on these can be picked up through tourist information centres located in the main towns throughout the region or the Bréifne website (www.breifne.ie).

## Safety

The clothing and equipment required will depend on the amount of time you plan to walk for, the type of trail and the anticipated weather conditions. It is advisable to have a waterproof jacket, proper footwear, food and liquid, a mobile phone in case of emergency and recommended safety accessories if taking the more difficult routes. Always check the weather forecast in advance of your walk and be conscious of traffic on public roads. It is also advisable to use a map to mark off your progress on the route. In emergencies

you should call emergency and rescue services on 999 or 112 and they will deal with your situation.
Finally, always respect the countryside and the people who live and work in it. Take litter home, leave gates as you find them, keep dogs under control, keep all water sources clean, protect against fire and never interfere with livestock, machinery or crops.

Most types of bike are available for hire

## Cycling

Cycling is also a marvellous way to see and experience

Bréifne. Once you have a bike, which can be hired locally, all the elements of a highly enjoyable break or activity holiday are at hand: accessible countryside, rich heritage, the gentle pace of life and the renowned friendliness of the local people.

The long distance Kingfisher Cycle Trail that loops through Bréifne is named after the bird long associated with the waterways of the local countryside. The fully signposted route passes through over 20 of the main towns and villages in Bréifne and follows flat terrain, gently undulating slopes and steep climbs along minor country roads. It is designed in a figure of eight to allow for long and short cycling holidays and the 370-km trail is suitable for seasoned cyclists, beginners, family groups or individual cyclists. It winds

Mountain-biking in west Cavan

Cycling along the coast at Mullaghmore

around lakes and islands, along rivers and streams and through forest and country parks both in Northern Ireland and the Republic of Ireland, passing through counties Cavan, Leitrim and Fermanagh. Along the way it traverses scenic viewpoints, winds through village streets, and circles historic monuments and attractive landmarks.

Holiday packages and a full list of bike-hire locally available can be obtained at cycletoursireland.com. The entire route is well signposted and can be followed easily. Accommodation is readily available in the range of B&B's along the route, and tailored breaks can also be enjoyed in hotels, hostels and luxury homes, where you can combine cycling with other activities.

As with walking it is important to ensure that the correct clothing and safety procedures are followed. Comfortable cycling clothing, waterproofs, helmet, and items such as sun cream, water and modest first aid equipment are all recommended.

## Useful Contacts

### Bike hire providers

**Fitz Hire**
Belturbet
Co Cavan
**T:** 00353 (0)49 9522866

**Wildflower Cycling**
Derryvaughan
Ballyconnell
**T:** 00353 (0)49 9523923
wildflowercyclingholidays.com

**On Yer Bike Tours**
Corleggy Farm
Belturbet
Co. Cavan
**T:** 00353 (0)49 9522219

**Declan Moran**
Moran's Bicycles
Convent Avenue
Drumshanbo
Co Leitrim
**T:** 00353 (0)71 9641974

**Marius Leonard**
Corralea Activity Centre &
Cottages
Belcoo
Co Fermanagh
**T:** 0044 (0)28 6638 6123
**W:** activityireland.com

**Kingfisher Cycle trail**
c/o The Greenbox,
Manorhamilton
Co. Leitrim
**T:** 00353 (0)71 9856898
**W:** cycletoursireland.com

Cycling is a great way to explore the secrets of the Breifne landscape

Walking in the Cuilcagh Mountains

# WATER SPORTS

Bréifne, with its extensive water systems and coastlines at Sligo and Leitrim, offers a wide range of water pursuits from surfing, skiing, canoeing and fun family activities to more demanding and challenging activities for those who enjoy the great outdoors.

## Surfing

The Atlantic Ocean provides great surfing at Sligo. Regarded by many as among the best surfing in Europe, numerous championship events are held there. With clubs in Strandhill and Drumcliff surfing is available to all, from absolute beginners to the very experienced. There is a surfing school and shop on the beach at Strandhill. Equipment may be hired and tuition is provided.

## Sailing

The natural beauty of the Sligo coastline provides a perfect location for leisurely sailing or inshore racing. Yachts from Sligo Yacht Club race almost daily during the summer months in Sligo Bay. Adults and children can participate in sailing courses or enjoy watching a sailing event at Mullaghmore Sailing Club on the north Sligo coastline. The lake systems in Bréifne, especially those of Lough Erne, also offer good sailing.

## Windsurfing, kayaking, canoeing, rowing

Outdoor adventure centres on Lough MacNean, Lough Melvin and Lough Allen provide instruction in and opportunities to enjoy windsurfing, kayaking, canoeing and rowing on the waterways. These are always enjoyable for the general visitor and can be designed as testing challenges for the more experienced.

## Canoeing on Lough Erne

The Lough Erne Canoe Trail is a first for Ireland with over 50km of waterway to navigate. It is suitable for all levels of abilities and begins at Muckross in Lower Lough Erne, linking with the Shannon Waterway and passing Cuilcagh Mountain. Interpretation panels dotted along the shoreline provide canoeists with information on nearby facilities, safety, the environment and local history. The upper lough is good for beginners while the lower lough is more suitable for the experienced canoeist. Further details can be found at the tourist office in Fermanagh.

## Swimming

Many lakes in Bréifne have dedicated swimming areas. Most do not have lifeguards on duty so caution should be exercised and signs always observed. If in doubt seek local advice. The Sligo coastline has many beautiful safe beaches such as at Rosses Point, Culleenamore and Streedagh. The beaches at Mullaghmore and Rosses Point both have Blue Flag status. If you prefer to swim indoors in a heated pool, there are pools in the hotels and leisure centres throughout Bréifne.

Water acrobatics in Enniskillen

Sailing on Lough Erne

Always wear the proper safety and flotation devices when enjoying water sports

Heading into the surf at Strandhill

# SPORTS

There is a wide range of sporting activities which can be enjoyed by visitors to Bréifne with a variety of traditional team sports that continue throughout the year. There are some tremendous championship golf courses and Ireland's finest caving systems for the adventure sports enthuasist. It is best to check local papers and your accommodation provider for details on upcoming events and local sports.

## Gaelic Athletic Association (GAA)

Gaelic games are the predominant sporting activity throughout Bréifne. Gaelic football is the most widely played game, and hurling, camogie and ladies football are also popular. The Gaelic Athletic Association is Ireland's largest sporting organisation.

Inter-county games are normally held on Saturday or Sunday and for most matches it is possible to pay upon entry. Club matches are keenly contested between the various parish teams and offer a great insight into the sporting life of the country.

In Bréifne GAA county grounds are located at Breffni Park, Cavan; Dr Hyde Park, Roscommon; Brewster Park, Enniskillen; Markievicz Park, Sligo and Páirc Seán Mac Diarmada in Carrick-on-Shannon. Inter-county matches take place at these grounds during the months of January to September but predominantly during the summer months from May onwards. The national finals take place each September in Croke Park, Dublin. Times and dates for matches are published widely in all newspapers.

## Rugby

Rugby is played by three clubs in Bréifne: Enniskillen, Cavan and Sligo, and they are all amateur teams. Rugby is also played in many schools and visitors can catch a match over the autumn and winter months.

Times and dates for matches are published in the local newspapers.

## Soccer

The only soccer club in Bréifne to play at a senior level is Sligo Rovers, which plays in the Eircom League. Rovers play their home games at The Showgrounds, Church Hill in Sligo city. Regular matches take place from March through to October each year and admission is payable upon entry.

## Golf

There is a wide range of top class and international standard golf courses throughout Bréifne. From the challenging links courses at Rosses Point and Enniscrone, to Strandhill with its ocean views and the

Bréifne offers the best caving in Ireland

The game of hurling is a unique part of Irish culture    The Ulster Championship is always keenly contested

championship parkland course at the Slieve Russell, golfers will find a variety of familiar and less well known courses to test their ability. Green fees, reservations and course information can be obtained by contacting clubs directly.

## Horse racing

Regarded as one of the most scenic courses in Ireland, Sligo Race Course at Cleveragh hosts race meets during the months of April to August. The programme comprises both National Hunt and flat racing. The racecourse is located less than a kilometre outside Sligo City centre just off the Sligo-Dublin road. Buses run every 20 minutes from Abbey St. It is a right-handed track situated on 56 acres overlooking Ben Bulben in the heart of Yeats country. For race times check with the racecourse. There are also informal race meetings on Culleenamore Strand in Sligo Bay. Check the local press for details. Roscommon also offers horse racing at the track just outside town.

## Caving

The carboniferous limestone and the large expanse of karst areas in Bréifne means that it is Ireland's primary caving destination. The Belmore-Tullyrack area north of Lough MacNean and the Cuilcagh Mountain area are two great locations, and the Reyfad Pot, Ireland's deepest cave system at 179m, is located here. Other significant systems are present in the high plateau between Glencar and Glenade. Caves are potentially hazardous places and it is strongly recommended that inexperienced visitors contact the Speleological Union of Ireland for advice (www.cavingireland.org).

There is a wide selection of great golf courses in Bréifne

All geared up and ready to go

Horse racing at Culleenamore Strand is a special
experience for lovers of the sport

# TRADITIONAL MUSIC

Traditional Irish music 'sessions' are commonly encountered in the pubs throughout Bréifne and they are an important part of everyday cultural life. Traditional Irish music is dynamic in form and although aspects of it have changed considerably over time it has a continuity that links the present with the past. Even in the modern world of digital media, traditional music is essentially still passed on from one generation to the next by singing or playing for a learner who picks it up by 'ear'.

Bréifne is recognised for a particular style of flute and fiddle playing and while these instruments are common you will also hear the uilleann pipes, tin whistle, bodhrán, accordion, concertina, mandolin, tenor banjo, guitar and bouzouki at the sessions.

The music as we know it today stretches back about 200 years, with the world famous blind harper, composer and singer, Turlough Carolan, recognised as the last of the

There is a long tradition of playing the flute in Bréifne

composers in the bardic harp tradition (see p50). In the eighteenth and nineteenth centuries Irish music was a solo, unaccompanied musical form. The only circumstance in which more

than one person played at a time was at dances. This was done simply to make the music audible. The stock of tunes in a given area may have been quite small, and knowing a tune that others did not could be a distinct advantage when one depended on this income as a professional musician. Many musicians therefore avoided performing in the presence of other musicians for fear that their tunes would be stolen.

Emigration in the eighteenth and nineteenth centuries provided the opportunity for the music to go 'international'. Among those who emigrated to the USA were James Morrison and John McKenna who played duets together and had a profound influence on later musicians. Another emigrant musician was the famous fiddle player Michael Coleman. Non-solo playing from musicians like these, and later musicians who recorded in the US, profoundly influenced the creation of the 'session' in Irish traditional music.

'Rambling houses' were homes where folk would spontaneously gather to socialise and sometimes to play music or sing or tell

The beautiful sound of the harp can be enjoyed at the annual Carolan Harp festival in Keadue

stories. New tunes were introduced to areas by members of the Travelling community, and musicians who had left their area would bring tunes home with them when visiting. The availability of Radio Éireann from 1930 onwards also gradually introduced new material to a wider audience than ever before and with the advent of programmes dedicated to traditional music from the 1960s, the store of tunes was spread nationally.

Comhaltas Ceoltóirí Éireann, founded in 1951, is the national organisation dedicated to the promotion of Irish music. Comhaltas created the county and national fleadh (traditional music and dance competitions and performances - pronounced 'fla') and organises annual county fleadhs throughout Bréifne during the summer months. Visitors can attend important traditional schools and festivals in Bréifne, such as the Joe Mooney Summer School in Drumshanbo, the Fiddler of Dooney competition in Sligo and the James Morrison Festival in Riverstown. The renowned Carolan International Harp Festival also takes place annually at Keadue on the August bank holiday.

Check locally for when organised sessions are taking place and also consult the local papers. Children are required by law to be off licensed premises by 9.00pm each evening. A cover charge may sometimes apply. The pub session remains a great experience and well worth attending.

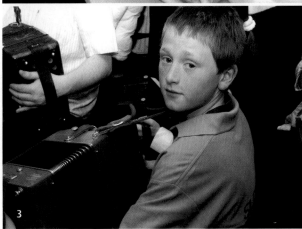

1. Irish dancing has hit the world stage in recent years and has always been popular in Bréifne  2. A bodhrán player in Ballinamore.  3. All ages can participate in a session.

The unique style of fiddle playing in south Sligo owes much to the influence of James Morrison

# CRAFTS

Traditional and contemporary crafts can be purchased at many locations throughout Bréifne. Crafts such as lace, pottery, glass blowing, print, table looms, crystal, stone and clay, tableware, ceramics, batiks, oil and acrylic painting, crochet, tapestry and embroidery, wood carving, knitwear, and fly-tying are all carried out at various locations. The following are a selection of the places where Bréifne crafts are exhibited and sold. The local tourist offices will provide details on the wider range of outlets.

**Leitrim Sculpture Centre**
[♿] Manorhamilton,
Co Leitrim,
T: 00353 (0)71 9855098

Contemporary and artistic crafts such as sculpture and ceramics are undertaken in the Leitrim Sculpture Centre which also provides training in sculpture and bronze casting. The centre maintains an artist in residence programme. Visitors can purchase work at exhibitions held regularly in the centre.

**The Buttermarket Craft and Design Centre**
[🏠][♿][♨][cc][P] Enniskillen,
Co Fermanagh,
T: 0044 (0)28 6632 4499

This centre houses over a dozen craftsmen and craftswomen in their various shops. The Buttermarket is a restored nineteenth-century dairy market with such diverse crafts as pottery, ceramic sculpture, watch-making, fly-tying and painting. Visitors are welcome to watch craft workers produce their goods. There is also a nice

coffee shop and store in the courtyard.

**Leitrim Design House**
[🏠][♿][cc][P] The Dock,
Carrick-on-Shannon
T: 00353 (0) 71 9650550

Offers visitors the best in contemporary craft, design and visual art with a selection of unique, handmade pieces from over 60 craft workshops on display. Crafts include furniture, interior items, books, accessories, handbags, gifts for children and jewellery.

**Cavan Crystal Showroom**
[🏠][♿][cc][P] Cavan Crystal Hotel, Cavan,
T: 00353 (0)49 4331800

The designs of the famous Cavan Crystal style of cut glass are on display in the Cavan Crystal Showroom. The showroom also sells tableware, furniture, textiles, pottery and ceramics, jewellery, wood, linen, iron craft, candles, sculpture, paintings and objets d'art.

Leitrim Design House

### Leitrim Crystal

🔊♿🎨📷cc📇€ Market Yard Centre, Carrick-on-Shannon,
**T:** 00353 (0)71 9622255

The proprietor of Leitrim Crystal is a master glass cutter and welcomes visitors to view crystal being designed, cut and engraved. A full range of gift and tableware is available for purchase.

### Bear Essentials

🔊♿🎨cc🖼️€ Bawnboy, Co Cavan,
**T:** 00353 (0)49 9523461

Bear Essentials teddy bears are inspired by Celtic mythology and culture. The bears are made from fine mohair and have fully jointed limbs. Visit the bear showroom, participate in bear-making classes, or watch as a bear is being created.

### Ben Bulben Pottery

🔊♿🎨cc€ Branley's Yard, Rathcormac, Co Sligo,
**T:** 00353 (0)71 9146929

The pottery produces a wide range of functional pottery and one-off ceramic pieces. Visitors are welcome to see the goods being made on the potters wheel and view the finished products in the showroom.

### Michael Kennedy Ceramics

🔊♿cc📇€ Market Yard, Sligo,
**T:** 00353 (0)71 9162586

The unique and original ceramic artwork of Michael Kennedy evokes all that is associated with the west of Ireland.

### Sheelin Antique Irish Lace Museum & Shop

🔊♿£cc📇 Bellanaleck, Fermanagh
**T:** 0044(0)28 6634 8052

The museum in Bellanaleck houses approximately 700 exhibits, illustrating the five

## Crafts of the land

The crafts which fashioned the implements and products for use around the farm are a vital part of Irish heritage. They usually had a practical purpose such as tools for farming, handspinning for clothing, musical implements for entertainment or furniture for use in the home. They all had their origin in a sense of self-sufficiency and the use of materials garnered from the land. The opportunity to witness these skills is becoming less available but at the annual Riverstown Fair the visitor can appreciate the delicate skills of the basket-masker and the iron working abilities of the blacksmith. There are a number of folk museums in Bréifne where a wide range of traditional implements can be appreciated.

main types of lace made in Ireland from 1850 to 1900. On display are wedding dresses, veils, shawls, parasols, baby bonnets, christening gowns and jackets. There is a wide variety of lace for sale.

### The Cat and Moon Craft Shop and Gallery
🏠 CC 🚻 € 4 Castle Street, Sligo,
T: 00353 (0)71 9143686

The gallery is a showcase for the very best in Irish jewellery design, fine art and hand craft. The first floor gallery features a new exhibition each month.

### Belleek Pottery
🏠 🚻 🍴 👕 £ CC P 🅿 🛈 🏧 €
Belleek, Co Fermanagh,
T: 0044 (0)28 6865 9300,

Belleek Pottery began making heavy earthen pottery in 1858 and has now progressed to become the highly acclaimed creator of fine Parian china known the world over. Visitors can take the pottery tour, or visit the showroom, museum and tea room.

### Christmas Craft Fair
🏠 🚻 👕 P € King House, Boyle, Co Roscommon,
T: 00353 (0)71 9663242

In November, a wide variety of crafts are on offer in King House. Crafts include woodcraft, pottery, candles, ironwork, as well as traditional Christmas decorations.

## Fly dresser

🏠 CC P 🅿 🚻 ☺ € T: 0044 (0)28 66323047 Enniskillen's Buttermarket Centre holds the shop of Frankie McPhillips, a professional fly dresser who, for over 20 years, has produced flies that are used by anglers worldwide. There are two main types of fly preferred by anglers; wet flies used underwater to simulate aquatic insects in their different stages of metamorphosis and dry flies which are meant to float on the water's surface and imitate adult aquatic or terrestrial insects that fall into the water.

The wet fly is often used to attract trout which spend a lot of time on the river bed searching for larvae, nymphs and snails. It is also very popular in early spring when the trout feed near the surface in fast water. The dry fly is popular between April and September when the trout are very active and feed on hatching or spent flies in or on the surface of the water.

Frankie's shop is also a great place to enquire about local angling news, boat-hire and to stock up on all your angling needs.

The tools of the trade for Frankie McPhillips, an expert fly-dresser

# RAILWAYS

Most of the railways in Bréifne were constructed after 1860, by which time the major national routes had already been completed. The railways played an important part in the lives of the people, linking far-off and nearby places and contributing to the development of towns and villages. These linkages served trade purposes such as the development of the Arigna Coal Mines and the access route to Belfast from Enniskillen for goods and produce. They also linked to the main lines for the annual GAA finals in Dublin's Croke Park - the highlight of many a person's summer.

From the nineteenth to the twentieth century, Enniskillen, Cavan, Carrick-on-Shannon, Boyle and Sligo - the main gateway towns of Bréifne - all enjoyed rail links but the once extensive rail network linking the towns of Bréifne with each other and the cities of Belfast and Dublin have now been closed and removed. Only the Dublin-Sligo route is still in operation.

Ireland's national railway gauge is 5 feet 3 inches, but many narrow gauge tracks were built in less populous areas because they were cheaper to construct. The first section of the three feet gauge Cavan and Leitrim Railway, from Dromod to Belturbet (54km), opened in 1887. It was the second last narrow gauge line in Ireland to close in 1959.

A major part of the railway heritage in Bréifne was the Sligo, Leitrim and Northern Counties Railway (SLNCR). Known locally as the 'Slow, Lazy and Never Comfortable', it provided the railway link between Sligo and Enniskillen and was Ireland's last privately owned common carrier.

After the partition of Ireland in 1921 the SLNCR found itself straddling two jurisdictions. The railway was never taken over by the state in either jurisdiction and in 1957 it finally closed when subsidies from both governments ceased. In 1951 a train journey from Sligo to Enniskillen took between two and two-and-a-half hours. The fare was five shillings for third-class return or 6/6d (six shillings and six pence) for a first-class return.

The Midland Great Western Railway line still runs through Bréifne today serving stations at Sligo, Collooney, Ballymote, Boyle and Carrick-on-Shannon and onwards to Dublin. This line was originally authorised in 1845 to link Dublin and Mullingar. The 82km stretch from Sligo to Collooney was never more than a single line and it only had one branch. At one time it had a branch from outside Mullingar to Cavan and a further branch off this from Crossdoney to Killashandra.

The small village of Collooney had a station for the Midland Great Western Railway - and two other stations, each catering for a different railway company.

## Sliabh an Iarainn Visitor Centre

T: 00353 (0)71 9640678

An interesting destination for railway enthusiasts is the Sliabh an Iarainn Visitor Centre in Drumshanbo. The centre features a wide range of displays and information on the area's close connections with mining and transport systems, including a replica of a railway ticket office; waiting room and many fine pictures of the railway.

## Cavan and Leitrim Railway

T: 00353 (0)71 9638599

Steam train rides can be enjoyed at Dromod in Co Leitrim. Trains run on demand, and on special occasions and the facility is open year round. There are tours of the site that will take approximately 40-50 minutes. They include a trip on the train and a tour of the engine sheds, workshops and the site in general.

Special events include the Vintage Day (May Public Holiday), the popular Hallowe'en night and the Santa special in December.

CAVAN STATION CABIN

Cavan Railway Station in December 1959
© National Library of Ireland

Ballyconnell Station in June 1959
© National Library of Ireland

# THE PLACE NAMES OF BRÉIFNE

Almost all place names throughout Ireland have their origin in the Gaelic language. A soft, rich and descriptive language, Gaelic has its roots in the long process of interaction between Ireland, England and north-western Europe. The language was in widespread use throughout Ireland from the fifth century and it is from this time that many of Bréifne's place names originate.

The Gaelic language provided a highly descriptive set of place names and this is clearly reflected in Bréifne. Descriptions of religious sites, battle sites, flora and fauna, folklore beliefs, geographic features, history and legend are all frequently seen in the names of towns and villages. For instance *An Cabhán* (Cavan) means 'The Hollow' and is suggestive of the drumlin country of east Bréifne; *Inis Ceithleann* (Enniskillen) means 'Ceithle's Island' – Ceithleann was the wife of Balor of the Mighty Blows, a local chieftain; *Cnoc na Riabh* (Knocknarea) is the Gaelic description of 'The Hill of Stripes' – probably a reference to fissures on the side of the mountain. The anglicised names in common use in Ireland nowadays are mostly derived from a combination of direct translations of the Gaelic description. Some names are very patchy translations, some have no direct connection at all, and small numbers of others can trace a connection to Viking influences and Norman-French influences.

Understanding the place names in Bréifne opens up a whole new way of appreciating the landscape. If you go beyond the anglicised version to the original Gaelic description a greater sense of place is suggested. In place names of Gaelic origin the descriptions of natural features are the most common. These include *sliabh* or mountain (for example, *Sliabh Dá Chon* – Mountain of the Two Dogs outside Fermanagh); *cnoc* or hill (for example, *Cnoc an Bhiocáire* - Knockvicar, in Roscommon); *gleann* or glen (for example, *Gleann Ghaibhle* – Glen of the Fork, Glangevlin in Cavan); and, *loch* or lake (for example, *Loch Mac nÉan* – Lake of the Sons of Éan, in Cavan-Fermanagh).

Others signify ownership or act as commemoratives. These include elements such as habitations or forts, ecclesiastic buildings, monuments or tombs, villages or towns, fords, weirs or bridges, roads, mills and kilns and so on. Then there are a number of place names linked with historical or legendary origins such as events, people, early saints, legends, fairies, customs, occupations, and agriculture and land divisions. While no apparent Viking place names survive in Bréifne, Milltown,

*An Bhoireann*, the Stoney Ground of the Burren Forest.

A traditional signpost with Gaelic and anglicised names

Gaelic name. Many townlands are also indicated on stone plaques by roadsides.

Those signposts will help to guide visitors around Bréifne. By recognising and appreciating the original Gaelic descriptions visitors can also enjoy directions and insights around the evocative and wonderfully descriptive world of Gaelic Ireland.

John O'Donovan, the scholar who undertook the research on Gaelic townlands between 1834 and 1841

Florencecourt, Riverstown, Rockingham, Hazelwood and Manorhamilton are all examples of English names, probably introduced by the Anglo-Norman landed gentry.

The largest category of Gaelic place names belongs to the 62,205 Irish townland names. The unique Irish concept of a townland originated in Early Medieval Ireland (c.500-1200 AD) and represented a basic landholding. Each county and parish was divided into townlands (called 'tates' or 'balliboes' in parts of Ulster), a pattern surviving to this day. Each townland averages 350 acres – an area large enough to contain a number of farms, whose owners were kin related and who traditionally co-operated to work the land.

Between 1834 and 1841 the Ordnance Survey, mainly through the work of the great linguistic scholar and historian, John O'Donovan, standardised and researched administrative place names and formed the anglicised

versions we see most frequently used today. Shortly after the establishment of the Irish Free State in 1921, the Gaelic language was encouraged and places revived their Gaelic names. Today most signposts throughout Bréifne display both the anglicised name of a town and its original

## Common components in Bréifne place names

| Gaelic | Translation | Anglicisation |
|---|---|---|
| Sliabh | Mountain | Slieve |
| Cnoc | Hill | Knock |
| Droim | Ridge | Drum |
| Mullach | Summit | Mullagh |
| Carraig | Rock | Carrick |
| Cloch | Stone | Cloch |
| Leacht | Flagstone | Lack |
| Magh | Plain | Moy |
| Gleann | Valley | Glen |
| Poll | Cave | Poll |
| Inis | Island | Ennis, inish |
| Tobar | Well | Tubber, tober |
| Ros | Headland | Rosses |
| Doire | Oakwood | Derry, dara |
| Eanach | Marsh | Annagh |
| Abhainn | River | Owen |
| Cluain | Meadow | Cloon |
| Rath | Fort | Rath |
| Caisel | | Cashel |
| Lios | | Lis |
| Cill | Church | Kill |
| Teampaill | | Temple |
| Baile | Town | Bally |
| Atha | Ford | Ath |

Image ©National Gallery of Ireland

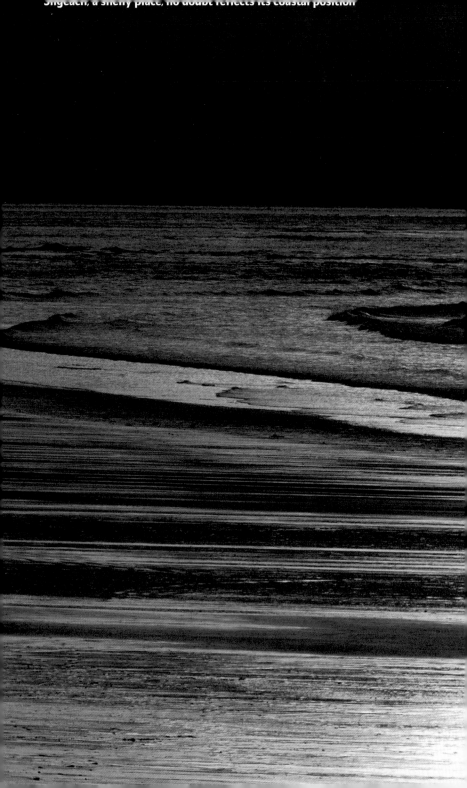

## Contae an Chabháin / County Cavan

| Contae an Chabháin | County of the Hollows | County Cavan |
|---|---|---|
| Ard Luachra | Height of the rushes | Ardlougher |
| An Babhún Bui | The yellow bawn (or enclosure) | Bawnboy |
| Béal Atha Conaill | Conall's ford-approach | Ballyconnell |
| Béal Tairbirt | Mouth (access) of the isthmus | Belturbet |
| An Blaic | The blossom | Blacklion |
| An Bhoireann | Rocky land | Burren, The |
| Droichead an Bhuitléaraigh | Butler's bridge | Butler's Bridge |
| An Cabhán | The hollow | Cavan |
| An Bhláthach | The buttermilk river | Cavan River |
| An Chláideach | The mountain stream or torrent | Cladagh River |
| Cloch Locha Uachtair | Upper lake stone (castle) | Clogh Oughter |
| Cros Domhnaigh | Cross of the church | Crossdoney |
| Binn Chuilceach | Chalky peak | Cuilcagh Mountain |
| An Dúgharrai | The black garden | Doogarry |
| An Damhshraith | The oxens' spread of ground | Dowra |
| Droim Leathan | Broad ridge | Drumlane |
| Gleann Ghaibhle | Glen of the fork | Glangevlin |
| Cill na Seanrathá | Church of the old ringfort | Killashandra |
| An Chill Mhór | The big church | Kilmore |
| Cill na bhFeart | Church of the graves | Kilnavert |
| Baile an Mhuilinn | Town of the mill | Milltown |
| An Abhainn Dubh | The black river | River Blackwater |
| An tSionainn | Sionann's river | River Shannon |
| Lag na Sionna | Hollow of the Shannon | Shannon Pot |
| Sliabh Roiséin | Mountain of the elder-grove | Slieve Rushen |
| An Muileann Iarainn | The iron mill | Swanlinbar |
| Loch Teampall an Phoirt | Lake of the church of the bank | Templephort Lough |

## Contae Fhear Manach / County Fermanagh

| Contae Fhear Manach | Of the Men of Manaigh | County Fermanagh |
|---|---|---|
| Béal Cú | Mouth of the narrow neck of land | Belcoo |
| Bealach na Leice | The flagstone pass or road | Bellanaleck |
| Béal Leice | River-mouth of the flagstone | Belleek |
| Botha | Huts | Boho |
| Doire Ó gConaile | Oak grove of the Connollys | Derrygonnelly |
| Doire Loinn | Flann's oak grove | Derrylin |
| Daimhinis | Ox island | Devenish Island |
| Inis Ceithleann | Ceithle's island | Enniskillen |
| Mullach na Seangán | Hilltop of the ants | Florencecourt |
| An Garastún | The garrison | Garrison |
| Inis Mai Samh | Island of the plain of sorrel | Inishmacsaint |
| Cnoc Ninnidh | Ninnidh's hill | Knockninny |
| Loch Mac nÉan | Lake of the sons of Éan | Lough MacNean |
| Loch Meilbhe | Meilbhe's lake | Lough Melvin |
| Maigh Niadh | Plain of heroes | Monea |
| Port Abhla Faoláin | Landing place of Faolán's apple trees | Portora |
| An Tulaigh | The hill/mound | Tully |

## Contae Liatroma / County Leitrim

| Contae Liatroma | County of the Grey Ridge | County Leitrim |
|---|---|---|
| Baile na gCléireach | Clerks' town | Ballinagleragh |
| Béal an Átha Móir | Approach to the big ford | Ballinamore |
| Beann Bó | Cow peaks | Benbo |
| Bun Duibhe | Mouth of the black (river) | Bunduff |
| Cora Droma Rúisc | Weir of the ridge of the tree bark | Carrick-on-Shannon |

| Droim Dhá Thiar | Ridge of the two...meaning unclear | Dromahair |
| Droim Conga | Ridge of the narrow neck of land between two lakes | Drumcong |
| Droim Caorthainn | Rowan tree ridge | Drumkeerin |
| Droim Seanbhó | Ridge of the old cow | Drumshanbo |
| An Duibh | The black river | Duff River |
| Fionach | Woody place | Fenagh |
| Loch Fhionnmhai | White plain lake | Garadice Lough |
| Gleann Éada | Eada's glen | Glenade |
| Gleann na nDamh | Glen of the oxen | Glenaniff |
| Gleann Buí | Yellow glen | Glenboy |
| Gleann an Chairthe | Glen of the standing stone | Glencar |
| Goirtín | Little field | Gurteen |
| Ceis Charraigín | Wicker causeway of the little rock | Keshcarrigan |
| Cill Fhearga | Church of St Fearga | Killargue |
| Coillte Clochair | Woods of the stoney place | Kiltyclogher |
| Cionn Locha | Head of the lake | Kinlough |
| Learga Uí Dhónaill | O'Donnell's slopes | Largydonnell |
| An Leacán | The small flagstone or discoid stone | Leckaun |
| Liatroim | Grey ridge | Leitrim |
| Loch an Scoir | Lake of the camp | Lough Scur |
| Loch Garbhros | Lake of the rough peninisula | Lough Garadice |
| An Lorgain Bhuí | The yellow ridge | Lurganboy |
| Cluainín | Little meadow | Manorhamilton |
| Inbhir | Headland or the river mouth | Rossinver |
| Sliabh an Iarainn | Iron mountain | Slieve Anierin |
| An Tearmann | The sanctuary | Tarmon |
| An Tulachán | The little hill | Tullaghan |

## Contae Sligigh / County Sligo

| Contae Sligigh | Shelly Place | County Sligo |
|---|---|---|
| Baile na Cora | Town of the weir | Ballinacarrow |
| Béal an Átha Fada | Approach to the long ford | Ballinafad |
| Baile an Dúin | Town of the fort | Ballindoon |
| Baile an Phoill | Town of the hole | Ballinful |
| Baile an Tóchair | Town of the causeway | Ballintogher |
| Béal Átha an Trí Liag | Approach to the three stone ford | Ballintrillick |
| Baile Easa Dara | Town of the waterfall of the oak | Ballysadare |
| Baile Uí Dhalaigh | Daly's town | Ballygawley |
| Baile an Mhóta | Town of the mound | Ballymote |
| Binn Ghulbain | Gulban's peak | Benbulbin |
| An Bricshliabh | The speckled mountain | Bricklieve Mountains |
| An Ceathrú Chaol | The narrow quarter (of land) | Carrowkeel |
| An Ceathrú Mhór | The big quarter (of land) | Carrowmore |
| Caisle Geala | Bright/white stone forts | Castlegal |
| Caiseal an Ghearráin | Stone fort of the gelding | Cashelgarran |
| Cliafuine | Hurdled thicket | Cliffony |
| Clochbhuaile | Stone boley (summer pasture) | Cloghboley |
| Calgach | Prickly place | Colgagh |
| Cúil Mhuine | Recess of the thicket | Collooney |
| Inis Uí Mhaolchluiche | O'Mulclohy's island | Coney Island |
| Oileán na gCuinigh | Island of the rabbits | Coney Island |
| Droim Chliabh | Ridge of baskets | Drumcliff |
| Droim Fionn | White/fair ridge | Drumfin |

## Contae Sligigh / County Sligo

| | | |
|---|---|---|
| An Ghráinseach | The grange | Grange |
| An Chéis | (Meaning uncertain) | Keash |
| Cill Mhic Treana | Mac Trean's church | Killmactranny |
| Sliabh Mór | Big mountain | King's Mountain |
| Cnoc na Riabh | Hill of the stripes (fissures) | Knocknarea |
| Lios an Daill | Fort of the blind man | Lissadell |
| Loch Arbhach | Corn lake (uncertain) | Lough Arrow |
| Loch Gile | Lake of purity | Lough Gill |
| Muine Dhúltaigh | Dualta's thicket | Moneygold |
| An Mullach Mór | The large hilltop | Mullaghmore |
| An Uinsinn | Ashtree river | River Unshin |
| Baile Idir Dhá Abhainn | Town between two rivers | Riverstown |
| An Ros | The promontory | Rosses Point |
| Sligeach | Place abounding in shells | Sligo |
| An Leathros | The half-promontory | Strandhill |

Florencecourt, or in Gaelic, *Mullach na Seangán*, (Hilltop of the ants)

## Contae Ros Comáin / County Roscommon

| Contae Ros Comáin | Coman's Wood | County Roscommon |
|---|---|---|
| Ard Carna | Height of the flesh | Ardcarn |
| An Airgnigh | The destroyer (reference to the river) | Arigna |
| Béal Átha Fearnáin | Ford approach of the aldergrove | Ballyfarnon |
| Mainistir na Búille | Monastery of the river Boyle | Boyle |
| Carraigín Rua | Little red rock | Corrigeenroe |
| An Corrshliabh | Rough mountains | Curlew Mountains |
| An Fheorais | Possibly refers to the 'spindly' nature of the river | Feorish River |
| Céideadh | Flat-topped hill | Keadue |
| Cnoc an Bhiocaire | Vicar's hill | Knockvivar |
| Loch Cé | Cé's lake | Lough Key |

*Cnoc na Riabh* (The hill of the stripes) with its ancient tomb site

Coffee and petit fours after dinner in the Radisson SAS Farnham Estate in Cavan

# ACCOMMODATION & DINING

Bréifne offers a wide range of hotels, guesthouses, farmhouses, self-catering and B&B accommodation. There is also a wide variety of cuisine and places to eat. Fine dining, organic food produce, themed food establishments, a wide selection of hotel restaurants, pub food, top class restaurants and more informal cafes, coffee shops and take-away style meals are all available. Pricing in the accommodation and dining sector reflects the nature of the establishment and special offers, weekend breaks and tourist menus are available in lots of places. It is recommended that you stay in approved accommodation throughout

Morning coffee and the newspapers in the Landmark Hotel in Carrick-on-Shannon

Bréifne. This is your guarantee that the property has been inspected and meets the minimum requirements set by the tourism authorities. Only hotels and guesthouses in Ireland are graded using a star system. B&Bs are located in towns and countryside and range from large period residences to modern bungalows. Further details on all of this can be obtained on www.breifne.ie.

MacNean's Bistro in Blacklion offers a fine dining experience

### Hotels

In addition to international hotel chains such as Radisson and Ramada, there are many Irish owned, large and small hotels in Bréifne. From a luxury four-star hotel with golf course and leisure centre to a smaller, more intimate family run hotel,

The Ramada complex in Drumshanbo is located on the beautiful shores of Lough Allen

## Hotel ratings

★★★★ Four-star hotels are of very high quality and are expected to adhere to very high standards and offer modern comforts. Accommodation is luxurious with suites and half suites available in most cases. Restaurant facilities are available with table d'hôte and/or á la carte lunch and dinner menus.

★★★ Three-stars range from small, family-run hotels to larger, modern hotels. Rooms are well decorated with the emphasis on comfort. All have private bathrooms with shower or bath or both. Restaurants offer high standards in relaxed surroundings with table d'hôte and á la carte lunch and dinner menus.

★★ Two-star hotels are generally family operated premises, selected for charm and comfortable facilities. All guest rooms have a telephone and most have a private bathroom with a bath and/or shower. Full dining facilities are available.

★ At one-star hotels visitors enjoy the comforts of a pleasantly simple hotel offering excellent value. These premises offer all mandatory services and facilities to a satisfactory standard, necessary for an enjoyable and relaxed visit. Some guest rooms have a private bathroom with a bath or a shower.

## Guesthouse ratings

★★★★ Four-star is the top classification for guesthouses in Ireland. Guest accommodation includes half suites and all guest rooms have private bathroom with bath or shower or both, direct dial telephone and colour TV and radio. Room service offers full breakfast. Many premises provide dinner, with table d'hôte and á la carte menus. Guesthouse facilities include car parking, safety deposit boxes, fax, newspapers and babysitting service.

★★★ All guest rooms have private bathroom with bath or shower or both and direct dial telephone. Guesthouse facilities include a TV lounge. Travellers' cheques are exchanged and at least two major credit cards are accepted. Restaurant facilities are available in some three-star guesthouses.

★★ Half or more of the guest bedrooms have private bathrooms with bath or shower or both. Guesthouse facilities include a reading and writing room or lounge area for residents. Restaurant facilities are available in some guesthouses.

★ These premises meet all the mandatory requirements for guesthouses and offer simple accommodation, facilities and services to a satisfactory standard. Restaurant facilities are available in some one-star guesthouses

Carnfree House, typical of many of the B&Bs you can find

The self-catering cottages at Benaughlin near Florencecourt

Bréifne offers outstanding choice. Most of the bigger towns in Bréifne have several hotels to choose from.

## Guesthouses

Guesthouses are bigger than B&B accommodation but smaller than hotels. Guesthouses must have more than seven but less than 30 bedrooms and are subject to the star rating system, whereas B&Bs are not. Lounge facilities with TV are available and most offer evening meals. Guesthouses are prevalent in Bréifne and offer high quality accommodation at affordable prices.

## Bed and breakfasts

The B&B is widely available throughout the region and has, for many years, been the cornerstone of accommodation throughout Ireland. Owners of B&Bs will be happy to provide you with local information and assistance to enhance your holiday experience. Many B&Bs also serve evening meals on request.

## Farmhouses

Stay in a genuine farmhouse and experience country living and nature at its very

Fine dining at the Olde Post Inn in Co Cavan

Farmers markets provide high quality, locally grown produce

Eithna's Seafood restaurant on the pier at Mullaghmore

## Premises without star ratings

Some premises will not show a classification in stars and these may be classified with the following symbols:

**U** The premises has decided to remain unclassified and will display a U rating. These premises meet all mandatory requirements for hotel, or guesthouse registration. **N** These are new premises that have not been operating long enough for standards to be fully assessed. **R** Premises undergoing major refurbishment at present. Classification will be assessed upon completion of the work. **P** Awaiting registration at present. **GR** Classification rescinded. At present the classification of these properties has been rescinded and is under review.

The unique charm of one of the bedrooms in Coopershill

Cromleach Lodge on the shores of Lough Arrow

The Cavan Crystal Hotel offers all the modern comforts

best. Irish farmhouses are excellent value and are perfect for families. Farmhouses can range from traditional homesteads to modern working farms. Farmhouse accommodation can be bed and breakfast (many offer evening meal also) and self catering.

### Self-catering

Numerous self-catering properties are dotted throughout Bréifne, ranging from chalets, cottages, and townhouses to apartments. Self-catering holidays are associated with freedom and independence and properties are often located in rural and incredibly scenic areas of Bréifne. See the self-catering section of www.ireland.ie for further details.

### Ireland's Blue Book

Ireland's Blue Book is a listing of luxury Irish accommodation in Irish country homes, hotels, castles and restaurants whose qualities combine

charm, style, character and individuality. Two premises in Bréifne have achieved Blue Book standard; Cromleach Lodge near Lough Arrow, and Coopershill House in Riverstown, both in Co Sligo.

### Hostels

There are three Irish tourist board approved hostels in Bréifne and all are located in Sligo. Hostels offer an inexpensive and flexible means of accommodation when touring west Bréifne. There is a selection of other hostels at various locations throughout Bréifne.

### Health and activity accommodation

Accommodation can also be combined with a health-farm break or an activity weekend. In many cases, the activity provider offers accommodation also. It may also be an idea to take the journey in your own hands and guide a barge or cruiser down the rivers and canals of Bréifne. Cruisers can

generally sleep between two and 12 people and can be hired at several locations across Bréifne (see p149, or www.breifne.ie for more details).

### Eco-friendly accommodation

In recent years, there has been a strong growth in ecologically friendly, low impact tourism in the north-west of Ireland. It is now possible to stay in tourist accommodation which has met strict environmental standards. Organic farming is becoming more widespread and many local B&Bs and guesthouses serve locally grown organic food. Further information is available on greenbox.ie.

Breifne has long been the centre of Ireland's organic food movement

# CRITICAL INFORMATION

Bréifne is located in Ireland's north-west and takes its name from the ancient Gaelic kingdom which was located in this part of Ireland. The region covers parts of Cavan, Leitrim, Fermanagh, Roscommon and Sligo.

You can travel to Ireland by air or ferry, and then on to Bréifne by car, train or bus. The Bréifne gateway town of Cavan is 110km from Dublin, 90km from Belfast and 97km from Derry and is well served with the N3 motorway. Enniskillen is 133km from Belfast on the A4 and 173km from Dublin on N3/A4.

The other gateway towns of Carrick-on-Shannon (150km from Dublin/230km from Belfast), Boyle (168km from Dublin/245km from Belfast) and Sligo (207km from Dublin/201km from Belfast) are all situated on the N4.

## By air

Fly directly to Sligo Airport from Dublin. Alternatively fly to nearby Knock Airport from Dublin, Gatwick, Stansted, Manchester, London and Birmingham.

Ireland is primarily accessed by air into one of its five major airports which are located in Dublin, Shannon, Cork, Knock and Belfast. The national airline is Aer Lingus which operates direct flights to the US, Britain and South Africa, as well as numerous destinations in mainland Europe. The other major airline in the country is Ryanair. Sligo Airport is in Bréifne while Knock Airport is close by.

## Ferry travel

Visitors from Europe can bring their own transport to Ireland or travel as a foot passenger via the six ferry-ports. The closest of these to Bréifne are Dublin Port, Dun Laoghaire, Larne and Belfast all of which serve ports in Great Britain. The ferry service from France serves Rosslare and Cork, in the Republic of Ireland.

You can visit the following websites for further information:

**P&O Irish Sea**
www.poirishsea.com
**Stena Line**
www.stenaline.ie

**Irish Ferries**
www.irishferries.com

**Norse Merchant Ferries**
www.norsemerchant.com

## Airports

**Sligo Airport**
Strandhill, Sligo
00353 (0)71 9168280
www.sligoairport.com
Direct flights from Dublin airport
8km to Sligo

**Knock International Airport**
Charlestown
Co Mayo
00353 (0)94 9367222
www.knockairport.com
139km to Cavan
Flights from London Stansted, Birmingham, Liverpool, Manchester and Dublin

**City of Derry Airport**
Eglington
Co Derry
0044 (0)28 7181 0784
www.derryairport.co.uk
112km to Belleek
Flights from London Stansted, Glasgow, Manchester and Dublin

**Donegal Airport**
Carrickfinn
Kincasslagh
Letterkenny
Co Donegal
00353 (0)74 9548284
www.donegalairport.ie
146km to Sligo.
Flights from Glasgow, Dublin

**Dublin International Airport**
00353 (0)1 8141111
www.dublin-airport.com
Flights from destinations across the world
120km to Cavan

**Galway Airport**
Carnmore
Co Galway
00353 (0)91 755569
www.galwayairport.com
115km to Carrick on Shannon.
Flights from Birmingham, Glasgow, Edinburgh, London City, London Luton, Manchester, Isle of Man, Malaga, Lorient, Paris, Dublin

**Belfast International Airport**
0044 (0)28 9448 4848
www.belfastairport.com
141km to Enniskillen.
Flights from UK, Europe and United States

**George Best Belfast City Airport**
0044 (0)28 9093 9093
www.belfastcityairport.com
144km to Enniskillen.
Flights from the UK and Cork

**Ballymote Railway Station**

## Train travel

Run by Iarnród Éireann (www.irishrail.ie), trains service the towns of Sligo, Carrick-on-Shannon, Boyle, Ballymote and Collooney from Dublin. Contact 00353 (0) 71 9169888.

## Bus travel

Operated by Bus Eireann (www.buseireann.ie) in the Republic of Ireland and Ulsterbus (www.ulsterbus.co.uk) in Northern Ireland, express buses serve the principal towns in Bréifne from Dublin, Belfast and Derry.

| N3 | |
|---|---|
| Béal Átha Seanaidh<br>BALLYSHANNON | km<br>105 |
| Inis Ceithleann<br>ENNISKILLEN | 52 |
| Béal Tairbirt<br>BELTURBET | 17 |
| (Muineachán<br>MONAGHAN | 49) |
| Droichead an<br>Bhuitléaraigh<br>BUTLERS BRIDGE | 8 |

Buses also operate between most of the larger towns in Bréifne. Bus Arás in Dublin is the central bus station for the Republic of Ireland while Europa Bus Centre in Belfast is central for the Northern Ireland bus system. Timetables are available from the tourist offices or from the bus offices.

## Driving

The roads throughout Bréifne are generally not congested and in many parts you may travel long distances without meeting any substantial traffic flows. Follow a driving route, details of which can be found in any of the local tourist offices. Alternatively enjoy the sights using the profiles provided throughout this guide.

Remember that driving in Ireland is on the left. Seat belts are compulsory for all occupants. Visitors to Ireland may drive using their national licence provided it uses Roman letters. Holders of other licences must also show an international driving permit in English.

## Parking

Parking meters and displays are used in the main town centres in Sligo, Enniskillen, Cavan, Carrick-on-Shannon and Boyle.

## Bus travel

**Bus Eireann**
Bus Arás
Store Street
Dublin
T: 00353 (0)1 8366111

**Europa Bus Centre**
Great Victoria Street
Belfast
T: 0044 (0)28 9066 6630

**Sligo**
Mac Diarmada Station
00353 (0)71 9160066

**Enniskillen**
Wellington Road
T: 0044 (0)28 6632 2633

**Cavan**
Farnham Street
T: 00353 (0)49 4331353

## Speed limits

Distance markers and speed limits are signposted in kilometres in the Republic of Ireland and in miles in Northern Ireland. There is a speed limit of 120kmph (70mph) in place on motorways in both jurisdictions. On dual carriageways the speed limit is 80kmph (50mph). Town and city speed limits are normally 50kmph (30mph) in built-up areas. Some roads in Northern Ireland carry limits of 60kmph (40mph), and in the Republic the limit on all regional and local roads (non-national roads) is 80kmph (50mph).

## Car hire

Most car hire companies will not hire a car to a person under 23 years old. Car hire can be secured through Hertz, Avis, and Budget Car Rental in most Irish cities and points of entry. Alternatively hire a car while in Bréifne from one of the following:

## Car hire

**Cavan Car and Van Rental**
15 Main Street
Cavan
Co Cavan
T: 00353(0)49 4361441

**Hertz Rent-a-Car**
Wine Street Carpark
Sligo
Co Sligo
T: 00353 (0)71 9144068

**Lochside Car & Minibus**
Tempo Road
Enniskillen
Co Fermanagh
T: 0044 (0)28 6632 4366

## Taxi and hackney services

Taxi ranks (queues) are available in Sligo and Enniskillen. Hackney and local transport services operate throughout the rest of Bréifne. Contact details for these services can be obtained in the local telephone book and tourist offices.

## Helicopter hire

Charter the Slieve Russell Longranger Bell L3 helicopter, which can seat up to six passengers, to travel swiftly for business or pleasure. For example, Dublin is only a 45 minute flight from Bréifne.
Slieve Russell Hotel and Country Club
Ballyconnell
00353 (0) 49 9526444

## Climate

Ireland has a mild, temperate climate with summer temperatures generally ranging from 15°C (60°F) to 20°C (70°F). Spring and autumn temperatures are generally 10°C (50°F). Winter temperatures vary between 5°C (40°F) and 8°C (46°F), but snow is a rare occurrence. Rain showers can occur at any time of the year. For further information contact Met Eireann 00353 1 806 4200 www.weather.ie, or the UK Met Office on 0870 900 0100 or 0044 (0)1392 885680 from outside the UK.

## Customs

Visitors to Ireland from the United Kingdom and other EU countries are not required to make a declaration to customs at their place of entry. However certain goods, such as meat and poultry are prohibited or restricted to protect health and the environment.

## Demographics

The population of the island is currently approximately 5.6 million, with approximately 3.9 million living in the Republic and 1.7 million in Northern Ireland. Ireland enjoys a rich diversity of ethnic groups and cultures and there is a dominance of young people; over half the population is under 30 years-old.

## Disabled travellers

Most public places, including visitor attractions, are accessible to wheelchair users, and an increasing number of hotels and restaurants are fully equipped to accommodate disabled travellers.

**Useful contacts for disabled travellers**

**National Disability Authority (Republic of Ireland)**
T: 00353 (0) 1 608 0400
www.nda.ie

**Disability Action (Northern Ireland)**
T: 0044 (0)28 9029 7880
www.disabilityaction.org

## Emergency numbers

In the Republic of Ireland and in Northern Ireland dial 999 or the European standard emergency number 112 from a mobile, payphone or landline for emergency police, fire service, ambulance, mountain rescue coastguard and cave rescue. The call is free but should only be used in cases of genuine emergency. On answer, state which service you require, wait to be connected to that service, then clearly state the location where the assistance is required.

## In the case of vehicle breakdown

**Republic of Ireland**
Automobile Association (AA)
T: 1800 66 77 88
RAC Motoring Service
T: 1800 535 005

**Northern Ireland**
Automobile Association (AA)
T: 0800 88 77 66
RAC Motoring Service
T: 0800 828 282

**Tourist Victim Support Service**
T: 1800 661 771
www.touristvictimsupport.ie
If unfortunate enough to be the victim of crime while visiting Ireland, the Tourist

Victim Support Service provides emotional and practical support. The service operates Monday–Saturday from 10.00am to 6.00pm, and on Sundays and national holidays from 12.00pm-6.00pm.

## Geography

Bréifne is an ancient kingdom and a geographically and geologically distinct region, part of which is in the Republic of Ireland and part in Northern Ireland. Bréifne encompasses parts of five counties: Fermanagh, Cavan, Sligo, Roscommon and Leitrim.

The island of Ireland is 450km (300 miles) long and 300km (190 miles) wide and covers approximately 84,500sq km (32,600sq miles).

Ireland is divided into four provinces: Ulster, Munster, Leinster and Connaught. Within these four provinces are 32 counties. The Republic of Ireland consists of 26 counties and Northern Ireland consists of six counties.

## Provinces and counties

The counties in the province of Connaught are Galway, Leitrim, Mayo, Roscommon, Sligo.

The counties in the province of Leinster are Carlow, Dublin, Kildare, Kilkenny, Laois, Longford, Louth, Meath, Offaly, Westmeath, Wexford, Wicklow.

The counties in the province of Munster are Clare, Cork, Kerry, Limerick, Tipperary, Waterford.
The counties in the province of Ulster are Antrim, Armagh, Cavan, Donegal, Down, Fermanagh, Derry, Monaghan, Tyrone.

## Health

Healthcare in all parts of Ireland is of high quality with modern diagnostics and treatment available. The accommodation establishment you are staying in will provide information on local hospitals and doctors. In an emergency it is best to go straight to the casualty (emergency) department of the nearest hospital with facilities.

### Republic of Ireland

Only short-term visitors to the Republic of Ireland from EU countries are entitled to free urgent medical treatment. Unless you are a UK national, you need to produce an EHIC (European Health Insurance Card) which you should obtain from your own health authority before travelling. Australia and the Republic of Ireland have a reciprocal health agreement. Australian visitors are entitled to receive emergency treatment subject to the normal charges for non-medical card holders in Ireland. In addition, Australian nationals are also entitled to assistance towards the cost of prescribed drugs and medicines on the same basis as those normally resident in Ireland. All other visitors to the Republic of Ireland

should ensure that they have adequate traveller's medical insurance.

### Northern Ireland

Emergency health treatment is free for all visitors to Northern Ireland, but if admitted as an in-patient then you will be liable to pay for further treatment. Free care beyond an emergency situation under the National Health Service is allowed only to UK residents and most EU nationals.

A number of countries have reciprocal health agreements with the UK including Australia and New Zealand. Visitors from other countries (including the US, Canada and South Africa) are advised to take out good medical insurance.

### Vaccines

No vaccines are necessary when travelling to Ireland unless you are travelling from an area where there is currently a notified infectious illness.

## Language
### Republic of Ireland
English and Irish (Gaelic) are the two official languages of the Republic of Ireland. Street and road signs are all bilingual. In Gaeltacht (Gaelic speaking) areas Gaelic is spoken daily but most people will also speak English.

### Northern Ireland
In Northern Ireland, English is the official language. The Irish language, Gaelic, is also taught in many schools and summer schools.

## Money

### Republic of Ireland

The Euro is the currency of the Republic of Ireland. One Euro consists of 100 cents.

Notes are €5, €10, €20, €50, €100, €200 and €500.

Coins are €2, €1, 50c, 20c, 10c, 5c, 2c and 1c.

### Northern Ireland

In Northern Ireland, Sterling is the currency, where 100 pence = £1 Sterling

Notes are £50, £20, £10, £5.
Coins are £2, £1, 50p, 20p, 10p, 5p, 2p, 1p.

### Credit cards

Any credit cards that bear the Visa, MasterCard or American Express symbol will be widely accepted in Ireland. Visitors with other cards should ask in advance or check if that card is on display where they wish to use it.

### Banks

Banks in Ireland generally open at 9.30am and close at 4.30pm Monday to Friday, except for Thursdays when they close at 5.00pm. ATM (cash) machines are located at most banks and accept most credit and debit cards.

## Pets

### Pets entering Ireland from Great Britain

There are no restrictions on animals being brought into Ireland from Great Britain. Special regulations apply to some dogs, for example, pit bull terriers.

### Pets entering Ireland from the continent

Pets can travel into Ireland without quarantine, provided they satisfy the requirements of the UK PETS Pilot Project. For further information regarding the conditions of this project in the Republic of Ireland, please contact: Department for Environment, Food, and Rural Affairs
T: 0870 241 1710
www.defra.gov.uk.

Further details for Northern Ireland can be obtained through:
Department of Agriculture and Rural Development
0044 (0)28 9052 4717
www.dardni.gov.uk

## Public holidays

### Republic of Ireland

New Year's Day, 17 March, Easter Monday, first Monday in May, first Monday in June, first Monday in August, last Monday in October, Christmas Day and St Stephen's Day.

### Northern Ireland

New Year's Day, 17 March, Good Friday, Easter Monday, first Monday in May, last Monday in May, 12 July, last Monday in August, Christmas Day and 26 December.

## Regional and national tourist offices

### Northern Ireland

Belfast Visitor and Convention Bureau
47 Donegall Place
Belfast, BT1 5AD
0044 (0)28 9024 6609

Fermanagh Lakeland Tourism
Wellington Road
Enniskillen
Co Fermanagh BT74 7EF
0044 (0)28 6632 3110
www.fermanaghlakelands.com

### Republic of Ireland

Dublin Tourism Centre
Suffolk Street
Dublin 2
00353 (0)1 6057700
www.visitdublin.com

North West Tourism
Áras Redden
Temple Street
Sligo
00353 (0)71 9161201

## Time zone

Ireland is on Greenwich Mean Time (GMT) and in accordance with daylight saving, clocks are put forward one hour mid-March and back one hour at the end of October. During summer it stays light until as late as 11.00pm but by mid-December it can be dark by 4.00pm.

## Smoking ban

The Republic of Ireland has a blanket ban on smoking in all places of work - this includes all bars, nightclubs and restaurants. Although hotel bedrooms may be exempt from the ban, it is applied to all other areas within hotels. In Northern Ireland a similar ban will apply from 2007.

## Telephones

### Mobile phones
Only digital phones with GSM subscriptions and a roaming agreement will work on the island of Ireland. Visitors should consult with their service provider before departure.

### Pay phones
Pre-paid phone cards are widely available both in the Republic and Northern Ireland and are convenient and cost-effective to use.

### Telephone codes
When calling Northern Ireland from outside the country all telephone numbers must be prefixed with 0044, and drop the 0 of the 028 local code. If calling Northern Ireland land lines from the Republic of Ireland, replace 028 with 048. For mobiles use 0044. When calling the Republic of Ireland from outside the country all telephone numbers must be prefixed with 00353, and drop the first 0 of the local code.

### Telephone enquiries
While in Northern Ireland directory enquiries: 118 500 international directory enquiries: 118 505

While in Republic of Ireland directory enquiries: 11811 international directory enquiries: 114. Other useful numbers can be obtained in the local telephone books.

## Visas, passports and embassies

Whilst UK citizens do not require a passport or visa to enter Ireland, most carriers by air or sea now require identification with photograph (usually either a passport or driving licence with photo). Visitors are advised to check what form of ID is required with the airline, ferry company, tour operator or travel agent before travelling.

Non UK nationals must have a valid passport or national identity card as appropriate.

Citizens living within the EU and many other countries including Australia, Canada, New Zealand and South Africa do not require visas.

All other countries should contact their local Irish embassy or consulate prior

to travelling to the Republic of Ireland, and visitors to Northern Ireland should contact their local British embassy, high commission or consular office.

**Embassies and visa contacts**
Further information for the Republic of Ireland, including a full list of Irish embassies, is available from the following:

**Department of Foreign Affairs**
00353 (0)1 478 0822
www.irlgov.ie

**The Passport and Visa Office**
**Irish Embassy**
Montpellier House
106 Brompton Rd
London SW3 1JJ
0044 (0)20 7225 7700

Further information for Northern Ireland is available from your local British embassy or consulate. For details please contact:
The Foreign and Commonwealth Office
0044 (0)20 7008 1500
www.fco.gov.uk.

# DISTANCES BETWEEN TOWNS

## (Km in colour)

| | Ballyconnell | | Belleek | | Blacklion/Belcoo | | Boyle | | Carrick-on-Shannon | |
|---|---|---|---|---|---|---|---|---|---|---|
| Ballyconnell | | | 44 | 71 | 28 | 45 | 37 | 60 | 27 | 43 |
| Belleek | 44 | 71 | | | 19 | 30 | 56 | 91 | 45 | 73 |
| Blacklion/Belcoo | 28 | 45 | 19 | 30 | | | 40 | 64 | 27 | 43 |
| Boyle | 37 | 60 | 56 | 91 | 40 | 64 | | | 10 | 17 |
| Carrick-on-Shannon | 27 | 43 | 45 | 73 | 27 | 43 | 10 | 17 | | |
| Cavan | 18 | 28 | 57 | 91 | 40 | 65 | 53 | 85 | 42 | 68 |
| Dromahair | 44 | 71 | 25 | 40 | 23 | 38 | 28 | 45 | 22 | 43 |
| Drumshanbo | 24 | 38 | 39 | 62 | 22 | 35 | 18 | 29 | 8 | 13 |
| Enniskillen | 19 | 31 | 25 | 40 | 12 | 19 | 49 | 79 | 39 | 63 |
| Manorhamilton | 47 | 67 | 15 | 24 | 14 | 22 | 42 | 69 | 30 | 49 |
| Sligo | 58 | 93 | 31 | 50 | 30 | 48 | 26 | 41 | 35 | 56 |

The main street in Boyle circa 1890

© National Library of Ireland

| Cavan | | Dromahair | | Drumshanbo | | Enniskillen | | Manorhamilton | | Sligo | |
|---|---|---|---|---|---|---|---|---|---|---|---|
| 18 | 28 | 44 | 71 | 24 | 38 | 19 | 31 | 47 | 67 | 58 | 93 |
| 57 | 91 | 25 | 40 | 39 | 62 | 25 | 40 | 15 | 24 | 31 | 50 |
| 40 | 65 | 23 | 38 | 22 | 35 | 12 | 19 | 14 | 22 | 30 | 48 |
| 53 | 85 | 28 | 45 | 18 | 29 | 49 | 79 | 42 | 69 | 26 | 41 |
| 42 | 68 | 22 | 43 | 8 | 13 | 39 | 63 | 30 | 49 | 35 | 56 |
|  |  | 64 | 102 | 38 | 60 | 32 | 52 | 54 | 87 | 70 | 112 |
| 64 | 102 |  |  | 20 | 32 | 35 | 57 | 10 | 16 | 12 | 19 |
| 38 | 60 | 20 | 32 |  |  | 36 | 58 | 23 | 38 | 28 | 46 |
| 32 | 52 | 35 | 57 | 36 | 58 |  |  | 25 | 41 | 41 | 67 |
| 54 | 87 | 10 | 16 | 23 | 38 | 25 | 41 |  |  | 16 | 26 |
| 70 | 112 | 12 | 19 | 28 | 46 | 41 | 67 | 16 | 26 |  |  |

Traffic on Grattan Street, Sligo in the nineteenth century

© National Library of Ireland

**Note:** References to main entries are in bold, those to illustrations in italic

# Acknowledgements

The publishers gratefully acknowledge the following people and organisations whose assistance and contributions made the production of this book possible.

The staff of Cavan County Council especially Des Maguire, Susan Monaghan and Siobhan Donoghue.

Jack Keyes, Rodney Conor, Hubert Kearns, Garth Earls, Peadar McArdle, Jackie Maguire, Danny McLoughlin and John Tiernan.

The staff of The Special EU Programmes Body.

Ignatius Maguire, Hughie Cullen, Joe Bradley, Frankie McPhillips, Seamus Lehany and George Morrissey.

The staff of the National Museum of Ireland, particularly Maeve Sikora, Isabella Mulhall, Paul Mullarkey, Aoife MacBride and Sandra McElroy.

An Dr Conchubhar Ó Crualaoich, Irish Placenames Commission.

The staff of the National Monuments Division of the Department of the Environment Heritage and Local Government, particularly Michael Moore, Eamonn Cody, Geraldine Crowley, Claire Breen, Tony Roche, John Scarry and Patricia Keenan.

The staff of the library of the Royal Irish Academy, particularly Petra Schnabel.
The staff of the National Library of Ireland and the National Photographic archive.
The staff of the National Gallery of Ireland.
The staff of the Environment and Heritage Service of Northern Ireland, particularly Brian Williams, Ken Neill, Robert Haddon and Tony Corey.

The staff of the Ulster Museum, particularly Patricia McClean, Sinead McCartan and Pauline Dickson.
The staff of the Ulster Folk and Transport Museum.
Margaret Kane of Enniskillen Library and Mairead O'Dolan of the Belcoo Historical Society.
Anna Harrison of the National Trust Photographic Library.
Gemma Thornton, Amanda McMullan and Shirley Morrow of the University of Ulster.
The staff of Cavan, Leitrim, Roscommon and Sligo county libraries, as well as Boyle public library.
The National Parks and Wildlife Service of the Department of the Environment, Heritage and Local Government

The Centre for Environment and Data Recording (CEDaR) at the Ulster Museum.
Birdwatch Ireland and IWeBS (Irish Wetland Bird Survey).
Martin Brennan, Dr Niamh Roche and Ian Herbert.
Irish Whale and Dolphin Group.
Tony Roche, OPW Photographic Unit.
The staff of the Roscommon Herald.
Ruth Murdy and the staff of Cavan Innovation and Technology Centre.
Conor Burns of Marble Arch Caves.

Neven Maguire and his staff at MacNean Bistro.
Darecha Flynn and staff at Arigna Mining Experience.
Christy and Maura Tighe at Cromleach Lodge.
Martin Byrne for his help on traditional Irish music.
Neil Armstrong and the staff of King House, Boyle.
Caroline Conmy and Siobhan Ryan of Sligo County Council.
The staff of Fermanagh Lakelands Tourist Office.
Rober Gibson of Fermanagh District Council.
Fáilte Ireland.
The National Trust.

The staff of Blake's Pub and the staff of Scoff's restaurant in Enniskillen.
Gerry Finneran at the Rainbow Ballroom of Romance in Glenfarne.
James McManus of Wildflower Cycling Holidays.
Gabriel Owens of the Forge, Ballinamore.

Mike Brown, Gareth McCormack, Robert Thompson, John Crellin and John McVitty for additional specialist photographic support.
Tom O'Dowd and Jerry Fitzpatrick
The staff of Belleek Pottery
Marie O'Reilly
Sile Garrett-Haran
Jim Nolan & West Cavan Committee
Killashandra Development Association
Erne Lakelands Tourism
Brian Connolly
Pauline Gilmartin
Ballingleragh/Boho Tourism Partnership
Arigna Leader
Wendy Swan at Kilmore Cathedral
Cavan Monaghan Rural Development
Noelle Sheridan
Irish Traditional Musicians Association
Ballinamore Angling & Tourism Group
Kiltycashel Development Company
The staff at Marble Arch Caves
Enniskillen Castle & Museums
Oliver Brady
The Irish Raptor Centre
Lough MacNean Tourism Initiative
Cavan Tourism
Leitrim Tourism
Heather Armstrong
Fermanagh Tourism
Sligo Tourism
The National Trust
Office of Public Works
Jim Chestnut

Seamus O'Toole, Seamus McLoughlin, Gabriel Miney and Gerry Knox